MENTAL HEALTH

FOCUS ON SOCIAL WORK LAW
Series Editor: Alison Brammer

Palgrave's Focus on Social Work Law series consists of compact, accessible guides to the principles, structures and processes of particular areas of the law as they apply to social work practice. Designed to develop students' understanding as well as refresh practitioners' knowledge, each book provides focused, digestible and navigable content in an easily portable form.

Available now

Looked After Children, Caroline Ball
Safeguarding Adults, Alison Brammer
Court and Legal Skills, Penny Cooper
Child Protection, Kim Holt
Capacity and Autonomy, Robert Johns
Making Good Decisions, Michael Preston-Shoot
Youth Justice, Jo Staines
Children in Need of Support, Joanne Westwood
Mental Health, Christine Hutchison and Neil Hickman

Author of the bestselling textbook *Social Work Law*, Alison Brammer is a qualified solicitor with specialist experience working in Social Services, including child protection, adoption, mental health and community care. Alison coordinates the MA in Child Care Law and Practice and the MA in Adult Safeguarding at Keele University.

Series Standing Order

ISBN 9781137017833 paperback
(*outside North America only*)

You can receive future titles in this series as they are published by placing a standing order. Please contact your bookseller or, in the case of difficulty, write to us at the address below with your name and address, the title of the series and the ISBN quoted above.

Customer Services Department, Macmillan Distribution Ltd
Houndmills, Basingstoke, Hampshire RG21 6XS, England

MENTAL HEALTH

CHRISTINE HUTCHISON
AND
NEIL HICKMAN

First published 2016 by
PALGRAVE

Palgrave in the UK is an imprint of Macmillan Publishers Limited, registered in England, company number 785998, of 4 Crinan Street, London, N1 9XW.

Palgrave Macmillan in the US is a division of St Martin's Press LLC, 175 Fifth Avenue, New York, NY 10010.

Palgrave is a global imprint of the above companies and is represented throughout the world.

Palgrave® and Macmillan® are registered trademarks in the United States, the United Kingdom, Europe and other countries.

ISBN 978–1–137–44740–1 paperback

This book is printed on paper suitable for recycling and made from fully managed and sustained forest sources. Logging, pulping and manufacturing processes are expected to conform to the environmental regulations of the country of origin.

A catalogue record for this book is available from the British Library.

A catalog record for this book is available from the Library of Congress.

Printed in China

CONTENTS

LIST OF TABLES

TABLE OF CASES

TABLE OF LEGISLATION AND STATUTORY MATERIALS

ACKNOWLEDGEMENTS

We are grateful to the colleagues and clients we have worked alongside in the course of our careers.

Thanks to participants, both in university and Edge training courses, for continuing to link law with practice and for asking challenging questions.

Special thanks to Steve James, Hazel Mackay and Mark Standing for their invaluable comments on the draft text and to Peter Hooper and Louise Summerling for their support and advice.

Finally, we would like to acknowledge the positive influence and support of Des Muller, Mark Barnard and Rob Brown, whose leadership qualities, humour and sense of humanity have shaped our professional careers.

Any inaccuracies within the text are ours, for which we accept responsibility.

ABBREVIATIONS

AA	appropriate adult
AC	approved clinician
ADASS	Association of Directors of Adult Social Services
AMHP	approved mental health professional
ASW	approved social worker
AWOL	absent without leave
BIA	best interests assessor
BME	black and minority ethnic
CAAPC	Commission on Acute Adult Psychiatric Care
CAMHS	Child and Adolescent Mental Health Services
CC	care coordinator
CCG	clinical commissioning group (England)
CMHN	community mental health nurse
CMHT	community mental health team
Code	Mental Health Act 1983: Code of Practice (England)
CPA	Care Programme Approach
CPN	community psychiatric nurse
CQC	Care Quality Commission
CRHT	crisis resolution and home treatment teams
CSSIW	Care and Social Services Inspectorate in Wales
CTO	community treatment order
DH	Department of Health
DoLS	deprivation of liberty safeguards
DSM	Diagnostic and Statistical Manual
DVCVA	Domestic Violence, Crime and Victims Act 2004
ECHR	European Convention on Human Rights and Fundamental Freedoms
ECT	electro-convulsive therapy
ECtHR	European Court of Human Rights
ESCs	The essential shared capabilities
HB	Health Board (Wales)

HIW	Health Inspectorate Wales
HRA	Human Rights Act 1998
ICD	International Classification of Diseases
IMCA	independent mental capacity advocate
IMHA	independent mental health advocate
IOP	Institute of Psychiatry
LA	local authority
LGO	local government ombudsman
LSSA	local social services authority
MA	managing authority
MAPPA	Multi-agency Public Protection Arrangements
MARAC	Multi-agency Risk Assessment Conference
MCA	Mental Capacity Act 2005
MHA	Mental Health Act 1983 (references are to the 1983 Act unless otherwise indicated)
MHAC	Mental Health Act Commission
MHRT	Mental Health Review Tribunal (Wales)
MHT	Mental Health Tribunal (England)
MWO	mental welfare officer
NICE	National Institute for Health and Care Excellence
NR	nearest relative
PR	parental responsibility
RC	responsible clinician
RCP	Royal College of Psychiatrists
RMO	responsible medical officer
RMP	registered medical practitioner
RPR	relevant persons representative
SB	supervisory body
SOAD	second opinion appointed doctor
WHO	World Health Organization

USING THIS BOOK

Aim of the series

Welcome to the Focus on Social Work Law Series.

This introductory section aims to elucidate the aims and philosophy of the series; introduce some key themes that run through the series; outline the key features within each volume; and offer a brief legal skills guide to complement use of the series.

The Social Work Law Focus Series provides a distinct range of specialist resources for students and practitioners. Each volume provides an accessible and practical discussion of the law applicable to a particular area of practice. The length of each volume ensures that whilst portable and focused there is nevertheless a depth of coverage of each topic beyond that typically contained in comprehensive textbooks addressing all aspects of social work law and practice.

Each volume includes the relevant principles, structures and processes of the law (with case law integrated into the text) and highlights clearly the application of the law to practice. A key objective for each text is to identify the policy context of each area of practice and the factors that have shaped the law into its current presentation. As law is constantly developing and evolving, where known, likely future reform of the law is identified. Each book takes a critical approach, noting inconsistencies, omissions and other challenges faced by those charged with its implementation.

The significance of the Human Rights Act 1998 to social work practice is a common theme in each text and implications of the Act for practice in the particular area are identified with inclusion of relevant case law.

The series focuses on the law in England and Wales. Some references may be made to comparable aspects of law in Scotland and Northern Ireland, particularly to highlight differences in approach. With devolution in Scotland and the expanding role of the Welsh Assembly Government it will be important for practitioners in those areas and working at the borders to be familiar with any such differences.

Features

At-a-glance content lists

Each chapter begins with a bullet point list summarizing the key points within the topic included in that chapter. From this list the reader can see 'at a glance' how the materials are organized and what to expect in that section. The introductory chapter provides an overview of the book, outlining coverage in each chapter that enables the reader to see how the topic develops throughout the text. The boundaries of the discussion are set including, where relevant, explicit recognition of areas that are excluded from the text.

Key case analysis

One of the key aims of the series is to emphasize an integrated under-standing of law, comprising legislation and case law and practice. For this reason each chapter includes at least one key case analysis feature focusing on a particularly significant case. The facts of the case are outlined in brief followed by analysis of the implications of the decision for social work practice in a short commentary. Given the significance of the selected cases, readers are encouraged to follow up references and read the case in full together with any published commentaries.

On-the-spot questions

These questions are designed to consolidate learning and prompt reflection on the material considered. These questions may be used as a basis for discussion with colleagues or fellow students and may also prompt consideration or further investigation of how the law is applied within a particular setting or authority, for example, looking at information provided to service users on a council website. Questions may also follow key cases, discussion of research findings or practice scenarios, focusing on the issues raised and application of the relevant law to practice.

Practice focus

Each volume incorporates practice-focused case scenarios to demon-strate how the law is applied to social work practice. The scenarios may be fictional or based on an actual decision.

Further reading

Each chapter closes with suggestions for further reading to develop knowledge and critical understanding. Annotated to explain the reasons for inclusion, the reader may be directed to classic influential pieces, such as enquiry reports, up-to-date research and analysis of issues discussed in the chapter, and relevant policy documents. In addition students may wish to read in full the case law included throughout the text and to follow up references integrated into discussion of each topic.

Websites

As further important sources of information, websites are also included in the text with links from the companion website. Some may be a gateway to access significant documents including government publications, others may provide accessible information for service users or present a particular perspective on an area, such as the voices of experts by experience. Given the rapid development of law and practice across the range of topics covered in the series, reference to relevant websites can be a useful way to keep pace with actual and anticipated changes.

Glossary

Each text includes a subject-specific glossary of key terms for quick reference and clarification. A flashcard version of the glossary is available on the companion website.

Visual aids

As appropriate, visual aids are included where information may be presented accessibly as a table, graph or flow chart. This approach is particularly helpful for the presentation of some complex areas of law and to demonstrate structured decision-making or options available.

Companion site

The series-wide companion site www.palgrave.com/socialworklaw provides additional learning resources, including flashcard glossaries, web links, a legal skills guide, and a blog to communicate important developments and updates. The site will also host a student feedback zone.

Key sources of law

In this section an outline of the key sources of law considered through-out the series is provided. The following 'Legal skills' section includes some guidance on the easiest ways to access and understand these sources.

Legislation

The term legislation is used interchangeably with Acts of Parliament and statutes to refer to primary sources of law.

All primary legislation is produced through the parliamentary pro-cess, beginning its passage as a Bill. Bills may have their origins as an expressed policy in a government manifesto, in the work of the Law Commission, or following and responding to a significant event such as a child death or the work of a government department such as the Home Office.

Each Bill is considered by both the House of Lords and House of Com-mons, debated and scrutinized through various committee stages before becoming an Act on receipt of royal assent.

Legislation has a title and year, for example, the Equality Act 2010. Legislation can vary in length from an Act with just one section to oth-ers with over a hundred. Lengthy Acts are usually divided into headed 'Parts' (like chapters) containing sections, subsections and paragraphs. For example, s.31 of the Children Act 1989 is in Part IV entitled 'Care and Supervision' and outlines the criteria for care order applications. Beyond the main body of the Act the legislation may also include 'Schedules' following the main provisions. Schedules have the same force of law as the rest of the Act but are typically used to cover detail such as a list of legislation which has been amended or revoked by the current Act or detailed matters linked to a specific provision, for instance, Schedule 2 of the Children Act 1989 details specific services (e.g. day centres) which may be provided under the duty to safeguard and promote the welfare of children in need, contained in s.17.

Remember also that statutes often contain sections dealing with inter-pretation or definitions and, although often situated towards the end of the Act, these can be a useful starting point.

Legislation also includes Statutory Instruments which may be in the form of rules, regulations and orders. The term delegated legislation collectively describes this body of law as it is made under delegated authority of Parliament, usually by a minister or government department. Statutory Instruments tend to provide additional detail to the outline scheme provided by the primary legislation, the Act of Parliament. Statutory Instruments are usually cited by year and a number, for example, Local Authority Social Services (Complaints Procedure) Order SI 2006/1681.

Various documents may be issued to further assist with the implementation of legislation including guidance and codes of practice.

Guidance

Guidance documents may be described as formal or practice guidance. Formal guidance may be identified as such where it is stated to have been issued under s.7(1) of the Local Authority Social Services Act 1970, which provides that 'local authorities shall act under the general guidance of the Secretary of State'. An example of s.7 guidance is *Working Together to Safeguard Children* (2013, London: Department of Health). The significance of s.7 guidance was explained by Sedley J in *R v London Borough of Islington, ex parte Rixon* [1997] ELR 66: 'Parliament in enacting s.7(1) did not intend local authorities to whom ministerial guidance was given to be free, having considered it, to take it or leave it … in my view parliament by s.7(1) has required local authorities to follow the path charted by the Secretary of State's guidance, with liberty to deviate from it where the local authority judges on admissible grounds that there is good reason to do so, but without freedom to take a substantially different course.' (71)

Practice guidance does not carry s.7 status but should nevertheless normally be followed as setting examples of what good practice might look like.

Codes of practice

Codes of practice have been issued to support the Mental Health Act 1983 and the Mental Capacity Act 2005. Again, it is a matter of good practice to follow the recommendations of the codes and these lengthy documents include detailed and illustrative scenarios to assist with interpretation and application of the legislation. There may also be a duty on specific people charged with responsibilities under the primary legislation to have regard to the code.

Guidance and codes of practice are available on relevant websites, for example, the Department of Health, as referenced in individual volumes.

Case law

Case law provides a further major source of law. In determining disputes in court the judiciary applies legislation. Where provisions within legislation are unclear or ambiguous the judiciary follows principles of statutory interpretation but at times judges are quite creative.

Some areas of law are exclusively contained in case law and described as common law. Most law of relevance to social work practice is of relatively recent origin and has its primary basis in legislation. Case law remains relevant as it links directly to such legislation and may clarify and explain provisions and terminology within the legislation. The significance of a particular decision will depend on the position of the court in a hierarchy whereby the Supreme Court is most senior and the Magistrates' Court is junior. Decisions of the higher courts bind the lower courts – they must be followed. This principle is known as the doctrine of precedent. Much legal debate takes place as to the precise element of a ruling which subsequently binds other decisions. This is especially the case where in the Court of Appeal or Supreme Court there are between three and five judges hearing a case, majority judgments are allowed and different judges may arrive at the same conclusion but for different reasons. Where a judge does not agree with the majority, the term dissenting judgment is applied.

It is important to understand how cases reach court. Many cases in social work law are based on challenges to the way a local authority has exercised its powers. This is an aspect of administrative law known as judicial review where the central issue for the court is not the substance of the decision taken by the authority but the way it was taken. Important considerations will be whether the authority has exceeded its powers, failed to follow established procedures or acted irrationally.

Before an individual can challenge an authority in judicial review it will usually be necessary to exhaust other remedies first, including local authority complaints procedures. If unsatisfied with the outcome of a complaint an individual has a further option which is to complain to the local government ombudsman (LGO). The LGO investigates alleged cases of maladministration and may make recommendations to local authorities including the payment of financial compensation. Ombudsman decisions may be accessed on the LGO website and make interesting reading. In cases involving social services, a common concern across children's and adults' services is unreasonable delay in carrying out assessments and providing services. See www.lgo.org.uk.

Classification of law

The above discussion related to the sources and status of laws. It is also important to note that law can serve a variety of functions and may be grouped into recognised classifications. For law relating to social work practice key classifications distinguish between law which is criminal or civil and law which is public or private.

Whilst acknowledging the importance of these classifications, it must also be appreciated that individual concerns and circumstances may not always fall so neatly into the same categories, a given scenario may engage with criminal, civil, public and private law.

- Criminal law relates to alleged behaviour which is defined by statute or common law as an offence prosecuted by the State, carrying a penalty which may include imprisonment. The offence must be proved 'beyond reasonable doubt'.
- Civil law is the term applied to all other areas of law and often focuses on disputes between individuals. A lower standard of proof, 'balance of probabilities', applies in civil cases.
- Public law is that in which society has some interest and involves a public authority, such as care proceedings.
- Private law operates between individuals, such as marriage or contract.

Legal skills guide: accessing and understanding the law

Legislation

Legislation may be accessed as printed copies published by The Stationery Office and is also available online. Some books on a particular area of law will include a copy of the Act (sometimes annotated) and this is a useful way of learning about new laws. As time goes by, however, and amendments are made to legislation it can become increasingly difficult to keep track of the up-to-date version of an Act. Revised and up-to-date versions of legislation (as well as the version originally enacted) are available on the website www.legislation.gov.uk.

Legislation may also be accessed on the Parliament website. Here, it is possible to trace the progress of current and draft Bills and a link to Hansard provides transcripts of debates on Bills as they pass through both Houses of Parliament, www.parliament.uk.

Bills and new legislation are often accompanied by 'Explanatory notes' which can give some background to the development of the new law and offer useful explanations of each provision.

Case law

Important cases are reported in law reports available in traditional bound volumes (according to court, specialist area or general weekly reports) or online. Case referencing is known as citation and follows particular conventions according to whether a hard-copy law report or online version is sought.

Citation of cases in law reports begins with the names of the parties, followed by the year and volume number of the law report, followed by an abbreviation of the law report title, then the page number. For example: *Lawrence v Pembrokeshire CC* [2007] 2 FLR 705. The case is reported in volume 2 of the 2007 Family Law Report at page 705.

Online citation, sometimes referred to as neutral citation because it is not linked to a particular law report, also starts with the names of the parties, followed by the year in which the case was decided, followed by an abbreviation of the court in which the case was heard, followed by a number representing the place in the order of cases decided by that court. For example: *R (Macdonald) v Royal Borough of Kensington and Chelsea* [2011] UKSC 33. Neutral citation of this case shows that it was a 2011 decision of the Supreme Court.

University libraries tend to have subscriptions to particular legal databases, such as 'Westlaw', which can be accessed by those enrolled as students, often via direct links from the university library webpage. Westlaw and LexisNexis are especially useful as sources of case law, statutes and other legal materials. Libraries usually have their own guides to these sources, again often published on their websites. For most cases there is a short summary or analysis as well as the full transcript.

As not everyone using the series will be enrolled at a university, the following website can be accessed without any subscription: BAILII (British and Irish Legal Information Institute) www.bailii.org. This site includes judgments from the full range of UK court services including the Supreme Court, Court of Appeal and High Court but also features a wide range of tribunal decisions. Judgments for Scotland, Northern Ireland and the Republic of Ireland are also available as are judgments of the European Court of Human Rights.

Whether accessed via a law report or online, the presentation of cases follows a template. The report begins with the names of the parties, the court which heard the cases, names(s) of the judges(s) and dates of the hearing. This is followed by a summary of key legal issues involved in the case (often in italics) known as catchwords, then the headnote, which is a paragraph or so stating the key facts of the case and the nature of the claim or dispute or the criminal charge. 'HELD' indicates the ruling of the court. This is followed by a list of cases that were referred to in legal argument during the hearing, a summary of the journey of the case through appeal processes, names of the advocates and then the start of the full judgment(s) given by the judge(s). The judgment usually recounts the circumstances of the case, findings of fact and findings on the law and reasons for the decision.

If stuck on citations the Cardiff Index to Legal Abbreviations is a useful resource at www.legalabbrevs.cardiff.ac.uk.

There are numerous specific guides to legal research providing more detailed examination of legal materials but the best advice on developing legal skills is to start exploring the above and to read some case law – it's surprisingly addictive!

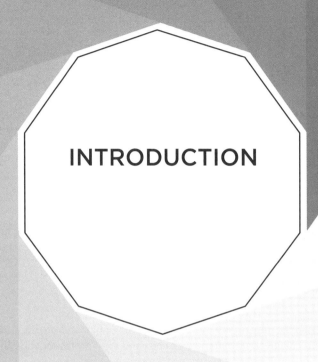

INTRODUCTION

AT A GLANCE THIS CHAPTER COVERS:

- ◆ definitions of mental health and mental disorder
- ◆ historical development of mental health law and policy
- ◆ review of the Mental Health Act 1983 and the 2007 amendment Act
- ◆ terminology
- ◆ chapter outlines

Social workers are involved in issues concerning mental health, regardless of their area of practice. Mental health is an area that raises issues of discrimination, individual and societal values, ethics and morals, all of which are core considerations for the social worker.

Social workers practise across boundaries. They may work in child protection but have to consider the impact of parental mental illness on child development. Hospital social work assessments may conclude that a physical health problem and mental health problem are inextricably linked. Social workers who liaise with schools will have experience of child mental health and the work of child and adolescent mental health services (CAMHS). Those working in the learning disability field will be aware that the recognition and diagnosis of mental disorder in this group is low but that the prevalence of mental disorder is high. Social workers supporting people seeking asylum may be faced with the impact of post-traumatic stress disorder (PTSD). Disorders such as postnatal depression, anorexia, anxiety or drug-induced psychosis could feature in any social work setting.

Social workers liaise with a variety of services and professions. Some of the key standards of proficiency for qualified social workers include being able to

- work appropriately with others;
- recognise the roles of other professions, practitioners and organisations;
- operate effectively within multi-agency and inter-professional partnerships and settings;
- understand roles, responsibilities and accountabilities of key colleagues as well as upholding their role and social work function in a multi-disciplinary context.

(HCPC 2012; Care Council for Wales 2014)

This book should prove helpful to social work students, in particular those in a mental health placement. It should also be helpful to social workers with an interest in mental health. It is hoped that in setting out the parameters of the law in relation to mental disorder, readers may be better equipped to understand both the powers and duties within the Mental Health Act (MHA) as well as its limitations in the reduction of risk and as a solution to complex social problems.

It is hoped that this text may also prove useful to a wider range of professionals who work in or have contact with mental health services. Policies, procedures and links to resources are integrated throughout the text. As the focus of the book is on mental health law, we acknowledge that exploration of wider practice dilemmas arising within mental health more generally, such as parental mental health, child protection, safeguarding adults and personalisation, is, by necessity, very limited.

Definitions of mental health and mental disorder

'Mental disorder' is the term that the current MHA uses and will be the term used in this text.

One in four working-age adults and one in six people of all ages experience a 'mental health problem' at some point in their lives, with at least half of people with a lifetime mental health problem experiencing their first symptom by the age of 14 (DH 2011; WHO n.d.). Terminology in the field of mental health remains varied and perplexing. Terms such as 'mental health problem', 'mental illness', 'disability', 'mental distress' and 'mental disorder' are a recipe for confusion about what health or ill health is. The World Health Organization (WHO) defines mental health as

> a state of well-being in which every individual realizes his or her own potential, can cope with the normal stresses of life, can work productively and fruitfully, and is able to make a contribution to her or his community.

The positive dimension of mental health is stressed in the WHO's definition of health as contained in its constitution:

> Health is a state of complete physical, mental and social well-being and not merely the absence of disease or infirmity.

Defining mental health problems becomes more difficult. In fact, there is no 'universally acceptable terminology' according to the Department of Health (DH) DH (2011). In its cross-governmental mental health strategy, it explains that the phrase 'mental health problem' describes

> the full range of diagnosable mental illnesses and disorders including personality disorder. Mental health problems may be more or less common, may be acute or longer lasting and may vary in severity. They manifest themselves in different ways at different ages and may (for example in children and young people) present as behavioural problems. Some people object to the use of terms such as 'mental health problems' on the grounds that they

medicalise ways of thinking and feeling and do not acknowledge the many factors that can prevent people from reaching their potential. We recognise these concerns and the stigma attached to mental ill health; however, there is no universally acceptable terminology that we can use as an alternative.

And mental disorders are defined as

a broad range of problems, with different symptoms. However, they are generally characterized by some combination of abnormal thoughts, emotions, behaviour and relationships with others. Examples are schizophrenia, depression, mental retardation and disorders due to drug abuse. Most of these disorders can be successfully treated.

The WHO lists a number of facts on worldwide mental health, including:

- Around 20 per cent of the world's children and adolescents have mental disorders or problems.
- Mental and substance use disorders are the leading cause of disability worldwide.
- About 800,000 people complete suicide every year.
- War and disasters have a large impact on mental health and psychosocial well-being.
- Mental disorders are important risk factors for other diseases, as well as unintentional and intentional injury.
- Stigma and discrimination against patients and families prevent people from seeking mental health care.
- Human rights violations of people with mental and psychosocial disability are routinely reported in most countries.
- Globally, there is huge inequity in the distribution of skilled human resources for mental health.

Mental health policy often focuses on the cost of mental health problems to society, estimated in 2011 at £105 billion in England (DH 2011). Such policies also acknowledge well-worn facts such as:

- The stigma attached to mental ill health, which leads to social inequality
- Worse outcomes in employment and housing
- Specific failures towards the black and minority ethnic communities
- The impact of unstable family backgrounds on the mental health of young people.

Each new government sets out its plans for addressing these issues with new strategies, for example, on social inclusion (Social Exclusion Unit 1997), recovery (DH 2009) and suicide reduction strategies (DH 2012a; Welsh Assembly Government 2009), to name but a few.

Despite the links between mental health problems and deprivation, it is important to note that mental illness occurs across all social classes.

Stigma associated with mental health problems remains high. The Time to Change campaign (2008) states that the stigma associated with mental health problems 'can be even worse than the symptoms themselves'.

Throughout the centuries, policy and law has varied in its approach to dealing with mental disorder, 'vacillating between an authoritarian and humanitarian approach' (Gostin et al. 2010). Different models of understanding have varied in their dominance, reflecting the views of society at any given time. It can be helpful to understand the historical context for the current MHA and reflect on whether it shows any great progress or change from its predecessors.

Historical development of mental health law and policy

The Royal Prerogative of 1324 (De Prerogativa Regis) gave jurisdiction over the property and affairs of 'lunatics' and 'natural fools' to ensure they were not exploited. Those with limited means would have been reliant on Christian charity or alms. There was no state provision of treatment or care.

In 1377, the Order of St Mary of Bethlehem Hospital (later abbreviated to Bethlem and colloquially known as Bedlam) established itself as the first hospital admitting 'lunatics'.

Various Poor Laws in the sixteenth and seventeenth centuries set to establish the relief available by classifying the poor into those deserving or undeserving of aid.

The Poor Law offered two types of relief, favouring support in the community by assisting relatives and the person to remain in their own home (outdoor relief). Indoor relief (usually a last resort) included local almshouses, hospital orphanages or the workhouse.

By the eighteenth century, institutions housed a range of paupers, orphans, the aged, criminals, vagrants, lunatics or the furiously mad (1713 and 1744 Vagrancy Act). From generally favouring community support, society turned towards institutionalisation. The notion of insanity developed along with the development of psychiatry as a specialist branch of medicine towards the end of the eighteenth century. However, treatment was based upon coercion and restraint. Records of public visits to the Bethlem Hospital through the eighteenth century document the use of manacles and chains. There was an increasing intolerance and segregation from the community with purpose-built institutions run by the State and private madhouses for those of means.

The York Retreat took a more humane approach to mental distress. Treatments such as beatings and confinement as well as underfeeding were accepted practices during the 1700s, but the Retreat was based on principles of compassion and respect. It advocated the real meaning of asylum as refuge, shelter and protection. The Retreat centred on Quaker principles and aimed to give control back to those with illness by treating them equally.

At various points, the law dealt with those with mental disorders (the insane, persons of unsound mind) and learning disabilities (idiots, imbeciles, mental defectives) in one statute. At other times, these groups were dealt with under separate laws and treated in separate asylums.

Alongside the development in asylum care, medicine and the medical profession were increasingly seen as the expert in this field:

> Madness is purely a disease of the brain. The physician is the guardian of the lunatic and must ever remain so.
>
> (*Journal of Mental Science* 1858, cited in Rogers and Pilgrim 2005)

The Mental Deficiency Act 1913 retained the categories of idiots and imbeciles but added 'moral defectives' who had 'strong criminal tendencies that required care, supervision and control for the safety of others' and 'feeble minded' who 'do not meet the criteria for imbecility, but it is so pronounced that they require care, supervision, and control for the safety of themselves and others'. The Act authorised the detention of moral imbeciles, who, for example, had children out of wedlock and were seen to be immoral in their conduct.

A new definition of mental deficiency was introduced with the Mental Deficiency Act of 1927: 'a condition of arrested or incomplete development of mind existing before the age of 18 years whether arising from inherent causes or induced by disease or injury'.

Previously, admission to hospital may have necessitated an application to a Justice of the Peace, but in the Mental Treatment Act 1930, a doctor could agree to admission if someone voluntarily wished to be admitted. This 'informality' was in keeping with an emphasis on treatment rather than merely containment. It can still be seen in s.131 of our current MHA, which allows for admission to hospital without any application, order or direction, that is, informally.

The Mental Health Act 1959 repealed all previous existing laws related to mental disorder. It reflected the perceived progress in psychiatric treatments such as electro-convulsive therapy, brain surgery, anti-psychotic medication and the belief that those with mental disorders should be treated in their communities where at all possible. Our current MHA has its basis in the 1959 Act. Mental disorder and learning disability were incorporated into one statute; however, promiscuity or other immoral conduct were expressly excluded as mental disorders in the 1959 Act.

The 1959 Act introduced the safeguard of the Mental Health Review Tribunal in response to the need for clearer and more robust safeguards to arbitrary detention. The other safeguards included a clearer process, replacing 'certification' with two medical recommendations and an application to the hospital by either a nearest relative of the patient or a mental welfare officer.

The current Mental Health Act 1983 retains much of the 1959 Act, although it introduced the role of approved social worker (ASW) to replace the mental welfare officer. It continued to allow for the detention of those with mental disorders, which included learning disabilities. The MHA has no lower age limit (with the exception of guardianship).

Prior to the 2007 amendments to the MHA, mental disorder was defined as:

- Mental illness (not defined).
- Psychopathic disorder: a persistent disorder or disability of mind (whether or not including significant impairment of intelligence) which results in abnormally aggressive or seriously irresponsible conduct on the part of the person concerned.
- Mental impairment: a state of arrested or incomplete development of mind (not amounting to severe mental impairment) which includes significant impairment of intelligence and social functioning and is associated with abnormally aggressive or seriously irresponsible conduct on the part of the person concerned.
- Severe mental impairment: state of arrested or incomplete development of mind, which includes severe impairment of intelligence and social functioning and is associated with abnormally aggressive or seriously irresponsible conduct on the part of the person concerned.

The additional test of 'treatability' applied to psychopathic disorder and severe mental impairment. The 1983 Act expressly excluded promiscuity, other immoral conduct and sexual deviancy, or dependence on alcohol or drugs from the definition of mental disorder.

In 1998, the Human Rights Act received Royal Assent and came into force in 2000. It incorporates various rights under the European Convention for the Protection of Human Rights and Fundamental Freedoms 1950 directly into domestic law. It also establishes that it would be unlawful for a public authority to act in a way that is incompatible with a convention right (s.6). As courts are required to 'construe all legislation (past and present) so far as it is possible to do … in a way which is compatible with convention rights' (s.3), this has a bearing on the development of law thereafter. See Appendix A for a list of relevant convention rights and case law.

Review of the Mental Health Act 1983 and the 2007 amendment Act

Since 1959, there have been frequent and significant changes in mental health policy and practice in the context of continuing advances in pharmacological treatments, the closing of Victorian asylums and an increasing emphasis on treatment and care in the community rather than institutions.

The legal and policy agenda in respect of mental health was also shaped by a series of high-profile cases. For example in 1993, Ben Silcock, who had a diagnosis of schizophrenia, entered the lion enclosure at Regent's Park Zoo, where he was badly mauled by a lion but survived.

The 1994 Ritchie Report into the care and treatment of Christopher Clunis, who killed Jonathan Zito, found Clunis to have been seriously mentally ill, but not receiving adequate follow-up. This led to a requirement by services to undergo a public inquiry into the care and treatment of any patient where a homicide was committed – a requirement that was vigorously campaigned for by the Zito Trust (founded by the widow of Jonathan Zito).

Michael Stone was convicted of the murder of Lin Russell and her six-year-old daughter in 1996. He had been known to probation, police and mental health services, and was reported to have a psychopathic personality disorder, problems with drug and alcohol misuse and a history of offending.

As a result of these developments, in 1998 the Government appointed an 'Expert Committee' to lead a root-and-branch review and to advise the Government on whether and to what extent the MHA required updating. This review reflected concern over public protection, in particular, the risks presented by people with severe personality disorder; the extent to which community-based services adequately met the needs of those with mental disorders; and how the MHA met the requirements of the Human Rights Act 1998. Compulsory treatment in the community remained high on the agenda. The MHA had already been amended by the Mental Health (Patients in the Community) Act 1995 to include aftercare under supervision (commonly termed 'supervised aftercare' (s.25A)) as a very swift response to the cases of Christopher Clunis and Ben Silcock above. However, in the views of some, it failed to go far enough in relation to the ability to forcibly treat the mentally ill in the community. There was a concern that people with mental illness, and in particular those who were likely to be 'revolving door' patients (DH 1993), required more robust supervision and care in the community.

The Expert Committee reviewed the statute and came up with recommendations for a new MHA in 1999 (DH 1999a). The issue of introducing capacity and personal autonomy to the criteria for detention was raised by the committee but rejected by the Government, which emphasised the need to manage risk, stating in their response to the committee:

> Concerns of risk will always take precedence, but care and treatment provided under formal powers should otherwise reflect the best interests of the patient.

> (DH 2000a)

In addition, there was an express intention to remove the 'treatability' test for personality disorder in particular and to legislate for the 'indeterminate but reviewable detention of dangerous but personality disordered individuals' (Jack Straw, Hansard 1999: 325, col 601).

The white paper 'Modernising Mental Health Services' was followed up by the arrival of the 'National Service Framework – Modern Standards and Service Models' (DH 1999b). In the foreword, Frank Dobson, then-Secretary of State for Health, introduced the policy as follows:

> Most people who suffer from mental illnesses are vulnerable and present no threat to anyone but themselves. Many of these patients have not been getting the treatment and care they need partly because the system has found it so difficult to cope with

the small minority of mentally ill people who are a nuisance or a danger to both themselves and others.

In 2002, the Government introduced a draft mental health bill including proposals for a wider definition of mental disorder and removal of the treatability test (thus to avoid psychopathic personality disorder potentially being excluded). Following scrutiny by the House of Commons, the Government went on to produce a new Bill in 2004, which the House of Commons and Lords agreed could proceed only if significant amendments were made. In 2005, the Government abandoned the Bill and introduced proposals to amend the existing MHA rather than draft an entire new statute. Meanwhile, the MCA 2005 received Royal Assent in April 2005, and in 2006 a further mental health bill was scrutinised. Following much debate and criticism from groups such as the Mental Health Alliance to previous proposals by the Government, they eventually introduced the Mental Health Bill in 2006, receiving Royal Assent in 2007. After all the debate and criticisms about certain proposals, the outcome was an amendment to the 1983 Act, to include the wider definition of mental disorder, with an appropriate treatment test for certain sections, the introduction of community treatment orders (CTOs), widening of professional roles in the Act, the introduction of advocacy (see Chapter 1), and introduction of requirements to provide appropriate environments for children detained under the Act. The concept of informal admission remained, alongside the use of the MCA where appropriate. As the 2007 Act was an amendment Act, the current MHA is still referred to as the MHA 1983.

Finally, one of the important additions in the MHA was the addition of the deprivation of liberty safeguards into the MCA. These were introduced via further amendment to the MHA because the Government had missed the deadline to include them as amendments to the MCA. These safeguards relate to Article 5 (A5) of the European Convention on Human Rights (ECHR) and the requirement that anyone deprived of their liberty by the State should have the safeguards of a 'procedure prescribed by law'. We shall look at this in more detail in Chapter 8.

More recently (and just prior to a general election), the Government published *No Voice Unheard, No Right Ignored – A Consultation for People with Learning Disabilities, Autism and Mental Health Conditions* (DH 2015a). This consultation reignited the debate regarding the place of learning disability in mental health legislation, and it proposes further reform.

As can be seen from this brief history, mental health law 'serves a shifting mass of conflicting interests and ideologies' (Hale 2010).

Terminology

Throughout this book there are references to the 'patient' or 'community patient'. The MHA uses this term to define those subject to the Act whether in hospital or in the community. 'Patient' is defined as 'a person suffering or appearing to be suffering from mental disorder' (s.145(1)) and 'community patient' as 'a patient in respect of whom a community treatment order is in force' (s.17A(7)).

The text uses the masculine gender ('he', 'him', 'himself') when referencing certain statutes. Older law, such as the MHA 1983, uses only the masculine gender. By virtue of s.6, Interpretation Act 1978, these statute references are to be read as including the feminine gender. More recent law, such as the MCA is gender neutral and uses 'P' to refer to 'the person'.

This book focuses on the law in England and Wales. Mental health law is different in Scotland and Ireland; there are also variations in the law and guidance between Wales and England, such as separate Codes of Practice and variations in regulations (see Appendix C). The book refers to the Mental Health Act Code of Practice guidance as it applies in England. The English Code of Practice (Code) has been recently revised and came into force in April 2015. At the time of publication of this book, the Welsh Code has been under consultation and is likely to be revised in the near future. It will be important to keep in touch with the revisions this will make to practice in Wales and any cross-border issues between England and Wales.

There is no doubt that change in mental health law and policy will continue, but whether changes to the law bring better services to those who need them remains to be seen. Those working in mental health services will understand the difficulties and demands of managing the elusive balance between social control, public safety and the human rights of one of the most marginalised groups in society.

Chapter outlines

The structure of the chapters is intended to broadly mirror the structure of the MHA, which follows a reasonably logical progression from dealing with definitions to the admission of patients under civil sections, to patients concerned in criminal proceedings, to consent to treatment provisions and safeguards. In addition, the particular complexities of the MCA/MHA are explored in a separate chapter. Each chapter refers to relevant case law.

Chapter 1: Professional roles

This chapter introduces the key roles in the MHA. Although there are no roles exclusive to social workers, the professional roles of approved clinician (AC), responsible clinician (RC), approved mental health professional (AMHP), care coordinator or independent mental health advocate (IMHA) are all possible roles for social workers.

Chapter 2: Mental disorder

This chapter introduces the definition of mental disorder and links with the ECHR and also explains the exclusions from the MHA definition of mental disorder and particular legal requirements relating to learning disabilities. There is also discussion in relation to children and young people. The concepts of ethics and models are considered, as are links in the MHA with capacity and consent.

Chapter 3: Civil admissions and police powers

This chapter considers the criteria and process for civil admission and the use of police powers under the MHA. The duties of the AMHP in respect of the nearest relative are also considered.

Chapter 4: Compulsion in the community

This chapter considers community treatment orders, guardianship and the use of extended leave from hospital, The recent changes to aftercare under the MHA by virtue of the Care Act 2014 are reviewed and recent case law concerning deprivation of liberty in community settings is discussed.

Chapter 5: Patients concerned in criminal proceedings or under sentence

This chapter considers the relevance of mental disorder at each stage of the criminal justice process, including the powers of the courts and the availability of defences to criminal charges. The chapter also includes the role of the social supervisor and the appropriate adult. Other relevant policy and legislation is considered.

Chapter 6: Treatment and consent

This chapter provides an overview of treatment rules in the MHA and instances where treatment can be given, with or without the patient's consent and the relevance of capacity. There are specific issues raised in relation to children. There is also discussion in relation to physical health conditions.

Chapter 7: Safeguards

This chapter considers the safeguards for patients within the MHA including the Mental Health Tribunal, hospital managers, independent mental health advocates and the nearest relative. The regulatory roles of the Care Quality Commission in England and the Care and Social Services Inspectorate Wales are also considered.

Chapter 8: Interface between the Mental Health Act and the Mental Capacity Act

This chapter considers the complex interface issues between the MHA and MCA including the deprivation of liberty safeguards (DoLS). It reviews the Supreme Court ruling on defining a deprivation of liberty and the impact of this on informal admission to psychiatric hospitals. There is also a review of capacity and competence issues relevant for children and young people.

Chapter 9: Conclusion

This chapter has concluding remarks and a brief discussion of the current and likely future legal and policy developments in mental health.

Although each chapter ends with a list of reading and relevant websites for further study, there are also several key texts and websites that are applicable across the whole book and are therefore listed here.

- *The Mental Health Act Code of Practice* (England) 2015 and (Wales) 2008 both have relevant chapters for further study of the MHA and best practice guidance.
- Jones, R. (2015) *The Mental Health Act Manual.* This comprehensive text is used by judges, solicitors and mental health professionals. It provides some invaluable notes and detail on various historical aspects of the MHA, accompanying statute and case law. It may seem inaccessible for those unfamiliar with its layout. See Appendix B for a guide on how to use Jones' manual.

- Wise, S. (2012) *Inconvenient People: Lunacy, Liberty, and the Mad-Doctors in England* (London: The Bodley Head).
- Liberty: www.liberty-human-rights.org.uk. An organisation campaigning for civil liberties and the promotion of human rights, Liberty provides some useful detailed discussion of human rights.
- www.mentalhealthlaw.co.uk. This free website offers regular updates on mental health, mental capacity and any related law. It also publishes annual reviews of all relevant case law. Joining is free and provides regular newsletter updates of recent case law decisions.
- www.mentalhealthwales.net. This useful website promotes choice in mental health and sets out the Mental Health Measure for Wales and a guide to service users and their families.
- www.mind.org.uk. This website has information leaflets and guides about the MHA which can be useful for service users and families.

Further reading

Books

Golightley, M. (2014) *Social Work and Mental Health.* This helpful overview of mental health policy, ethics, values and law is practice based and offers an introduction to mental health and related law for those less familiar with the field.

Pilgrim, D. (2009) *Key Concepts in Mental Health.* This comprehensive text explores various theories of mental health and illness, the structure of mental health services and, in particular, social perspectives of understanding.

Websites

www.mentalhealthandwellbeing.eu. In 2013, a Joint Action Mental Health and Well-being strategy was launched. This website gives details and links to other areas in the EU website on mental health. It does not focus on mental health law, but on policy and well-being across Europe.

www.kingsfund.org.uk. The King's Fund (2014) – 'Ideas that change health care – service transformation – lessons from mental health'. This website provides a helpful overview of the changes to mental health services, historical perspectives and discussion points for future mental health care.

www.time-to-change.org.uk. This website of a mental health charity is focused on ending discrimination and stigma caused by mental health problems.

www.museumofthemind.org.uk. This website of the Bethlem Royal Hospital's museum at the Bethlem Hospital is an archive of historical information on the care and treatment of mental illness.

www.studymore.org.uk. Offering an extensive library of key periods in the development of mental health law and policy, this resource has helpful links to other sites.

www.nhs.uk. With information about the NHS in England and the NHS structure, this leaflet 'Understanding the new NHS' is available in PDF format from this site and explains the role of clinical commissioning groups, NHS Mental Health Trusts and the Department of Health (DH).

www.wales.nhs.uk. This site gives information about NHS services in Wales that are devolved.

1

PROFESSIONAL ROLES

AT A GLANCE THIS CHAPTER COVERS:

- professional roles in the Mental Health Act 1983
- the approved mental health professional (AMHP)
- the police and courts
- the approved clinician (AC) and responsible clinician (RC)
- the independent mental health advocate (IMHA)

Professional roles in the Mental Health Act 1983

There are a range of professional duties and powers in the operation of the MHA 1983, including specific roles for assessing doctors and approved mental health professionals (AMHPs), police and the courts, prior to, during and after admission to hospital as well as in community settings. The 2007 MHA amendments introduced the role of independent mental health advocate (IMHA) for patients subject to certain sections of the Act. The Act also covers the role of relatives, specifically the nearest relative (NR) and their important powers and rights under the Act, which are discussed in later chapters along with the roles of the Care Quality Commission (CQC), Care and Social Services Inspectorate in Wales (CSSIW), hospital managers and second opinion appointed doctors (SOADs).

The roles above form part of a wider range of safeguards designed to both prevent arbitrary decisions being made by one person and provide scrutiny and regulation on the use of the Act and support to those subject to the MHA provisions.

The professional roles that are the focus of this chapter include the roles of the AMHP, AC, RC and IMHA. The precursors to these roles go back several hundred years, and many of the current duties and powers are recognisable from earlier statutes.

The approved mental health professional (AMHP)

The role of the approved social worker (ASW) was exclusive to social workers, but the 2007 MHA amendments widened these roles to a range of qualified professions based upon a set of regulatory competencies (Mental Health (AMHP) Regulations 2008). Although the majority of AMHPs are social workers (81 per cent of trainee AMHPs were social workers in 2011–12 [Jones et al. 2012, cited in Moriarty et al. 2015]), other professionals may take on the role, having successfully completed the appropriate training and having approval to act as such by a local authority. The following professionals as well as registered social workers can now be AMHPs:

- Registered first-level mental health or learning disabilities nurses
- Registered occupational therapists
- Chartered psychologists

Note that medical doctors are excluded from becoming AMHPs.

AMHPs have a range of powers and duties, as set out below. Essentially they are the key decision-makers around the need for compulsion, either in hospital or in the community, and have skills and expertise in making assessments and judgements affecting human rights. Their role is to provide a social perspective to balance the medical/psychiatric view, long held dominant in mental health services (Rogers and Pilgrim 2005). They must be independent of the detaining or responsible authority and therefore are approved to act by a local authority even where they are working within the NHS (s.145(1AC)).

On-the-spot question	Why do you think medical doctors are excluded from training to be AMHPs?

During the progress of the MHA 2007 through Parliament, there were debates about the ability of health professionals to be independent enough of doctors to take on the role of AMHP and assert a social perspective. However, the explanatory notes to the MHA 2007 (para 64) state that

> a wider group of professionals, such as nurses, occupational therapists and chartered psychologists will be able to carry out the ASW's functions as long as individuals have the right skills, experience and training, and are approved by an LSSA to do so . . . This does not prevent all those involved from being employed by the NHS, but the skills and training required of AMHPs aim to ensure that they provide an independent social perspective.

Independence is one of the key AMHP competencies in the English (5a) and Welsh (5.1) Regulations:

> the ability to assert a social perspective in decision-making and to make properly informed, independent decisions.

Many AMHPs may also be care coordinators (CC), a role originating with the Care Programme Approach (CPA) (DH 1990; DH 2008/Mental Health Wales Measure, Part 2, 2010), to coordinate the care of those with mental disorder in secondary or tertiary services. This is not a statutory role, and research suggests that clients are most likely seen by a health professional CC rather than a social worker CC (CQC 2015a). AMHPs may find themselves liaising closely with care coordinators to gather necessary information in relation to assessments under the Act. Guidance in the Code of Practice refers to the CC at various points, in particular in chapter 34.

Training for AMHPs

The Health Care Professionals Council in England and the Care Council for Wales are responsible for the registration and accreditation of AMHP qualifying courses. Some courses integrate the role of Best Interests Assessor under the DoLS within the training but, in any case, the AMHP is expected to have a sound understanding of the interface issues between the MCA and MHA as well as an understanding of deprivation of liberty and human rights.

Approval of AMHPs

Section 114 MHA states that a local social services authority (LSSA) may approve a person to act as an AMHP, but before such approval the LSSA shall be satisfied that this person has appropriate competence in dealing with people who are suffering from mental disorder. The competencies are set out in regulations and must be evidenced by the AMHP in his or her initial training and for re-approval (see Appendix C).

Although AMHPs act on behalf of and are authorised by an LSSA, they are autonomous and must act in their own right. They cannot be pressured to make an application for compulsion by the local authority or anyone else for that matter:

> Although AMHPs act on behalf of a local authority, they cannot be told by the local authority or anyone else whether or not to make an application. They must exercise their own judgement, based on social and medical evidence, when deciding whether to apply for a patient to be detained under the Act.
>
> (para 14.52)

Approval runs for five years, and LSSAs will have local arrangements in place to ensure that AMHPs working on their behalf remain competent to practise prior to re-approval. This includes the statutory requirement to undertake 18 hours of relevant training in each year that they work as an AMHP.

Duties and powers of AMHPs

Although the role of the AMHP has now superseded the ASW role, there are many similarities in the tasks and the complexities of both roles. As Manthorpe and Rapapport (2008) state:

> The ASW role is complex: it contains tensions inherent in following social control and empowerment objectives and meeting

service user and carer perspectives that may conflict. Regard has to be made to complex case law while simultaneously operating as advocate and assessor.

The AMHP role has become increasingly complex with the introduction of the Mental Capacity Act 2005 (MCA), professional obligations arising from the European Convention on Human Rights (ECHR) and the Human Rights Act 1998 (HRA), the interface between the MCA and the MHA/DoLS, and statute and policies in relation to safeguarding children and adults.

The AMHP is a public authority for the purposes of the Human Rights Act (HRA) (s.6) and has been described by Brown (2013) as someone who needs to 'show an awareness of relevant law and procedures and, in particular, as public authorities, a good grasp of and commitment to, the European Convention on Human Rights.'

Below is a summary of the main AMHP functions based on those set out in New Roles Guidance (NIMHE 2008) and chapter 30 of the Reference Guide to the MHA (DH 2015), with some additions.

Table 1.1: AMHP Functions

Reference	AMHP Functions
Section 115	Enter and inspect premises in which a mentally disordered person is living, if the AMHP has reasonable cause to believe that the patient is not under proper care.
Section 135	Apply for a warrant for police to enter specified premises to search for and, if thought fit, remove a patient, to a place of safety (see Chapter 3).
Section 136	Interview a person removed to a place of safety and make any arrangements necessary for his or her treatment or care or make a decision on transfer to another place of safety (see Chapter 3).
Section 13(1)	Consider the case of a patient when directed to do so by the LSSA for application for detention or guardianship under Part II of the Act.
Section 11(3) & (4)	Inform the nearest relative about an application for s.2 and his or her rights in s.23. Consult the NR for applications for s.3 or guardianship.

Table 1.1: *Continued*

Reference	AMHP Functions
Section 13(2)	Interview in a suitable manner and satisfy himself that detention in hospital is in all the circumstances of the case the most appropriate way of providing the care and medical treatment of which the patient stands in need.
Section 13(1A)	Have regard to any wishes expressed by relatives and any other relevant circumstances, and make an application if they are of the opinion that it is necessary or proper to do so.
Section 13(4)	Respond to a request from a NR for assessment under the Act and give reasons in writing to the NR if an application is not made.
Section 14	Provide social circumstances reports for patients detained on the basis of a NR application.
Section 6(1)	Take and convey to hospital on the basis of an application.
Section 137	Have all the powers of a constable for the purposes of taking or conveying the patient.
Section 138	Have the power to retake a patient following the patient escaping from legal custody.
Section 18(1)	Have the power to take into custody a patient who is absent without leave, and return that patient to the hospital or place where he or she is required to reside.
Section 17A	Agree (or not) to the making of a community treatment order (CTO) (s.17A) and any conditions to be included (s.17B) revocation of the CTO (s.17F) or extension of CTO (s.20A).
Section 29	Make application to the county court for the appointment of an acting NR.
Section 21B	Be consulted before an appropriate practitioner makes a report under section 21B confirming the detention or CTO of a patient who has been absent without leave for more than 28 days.
Section 47 Care Act & Section 58 Social Services & Wellbeing (Wales) Act 2014	Protect any moveable property of the patient if they are admitted to hospital.

Importantly, as we shall see in Chapters 3 and 4, it is the AMHP who makes the application for admission to hospital for detention in Part II of the Act, and agrees or not to the making of a CTO, or applications for guardianship. The assessing doctors recommend but the AMHP has the final decision-making power. This makes the role quasi-judicial and unique because AMHPs decide in their own right without the need for recourse to the courts.

The Code of Practice

The MHA sets out the duties and powers of the AMHP (and others) but the Code provides statutory guidance on how to apply the Act in practice.

S.118 imposes a duty on the Secretary of State and Welsh ministers to prepare a Code to guide certain professionals involved in the use of the Act. AMHPs, doctors and others, such as mental health trust staff, are required to have regard to the Code, and although it does not have the same status as law, it is statutory guidance, and any departure from it must be for 'cogent reasons' – *R (Munjaz) v Mersey Care NHS Trust* [2005]). The Code can be useful for others who are involved in the use of the Act such as police and ambulance services, clinical commissioning groups (CCGs) (or health boards in Wales), but it is not statutory guidance for them.

The Code clarifies that overall responsibility for coordinating the process of an assessment under Part II of the MHA should be with the AMHP (para 14.41).

The Code starts with a set of principles at para 1.1:

- Least restrictive option and maximising independence
- Empowerment and involvement
- Respect and dignity
- Purpose and effectiveness
- Efficiency and equity

Perhaps the most problematic principle is the 'least restrictive option and maximising independence'. The Code emphasises the role of the AMHP in upholding this principle at para 14.52:

> The role of AMHP is to provide an independent decision about whether or not there are alternatives to detention under the Act, bringing a social perspective to bear on their decision and taking account of the least restrictive option and maximising independence guiding principle.

However, the reality is of limited, if any, access to alternatives to admission at times of crisis, or timely access to appropriate beds where necessary (CQC 2015b; Community Care 2014; House of Commons Health Committee 2013; DH 2014a).

Government strategies and statutes such as the Mental Health (Wales) Measure 2010 and the Department of Health's *Achieving Better Access to Mental Health Services by 2020* (2014b) have targets to promote mental health and well-being. These aim to prevent mental ill health at an early stage and improve outcomes for those with mental health problems, enabling their quality of life to be improved. Both refer to 'parity of esteem' between physical health and mental health, meaning equal access to psychiatric crisis services where necessary and to timely and appropriate interventions.

The Care Act 2014 duty to promote well-being (s.1), provide preventative services (s.2), involve the person in his or her assessment and provide statutory advocacy, may strengthen the aims listed above. The Social Services and Well-being (Wales) Act 2014 reflects similar duties in the promotion of well-being (ss.4–7) and preventative services (ss.14–15).

However, against these ideals, detention rates under the MHA in England increased by 30 per cent between 2003 and 2013 at a rate that was greater pro rata than the general increase in the population (HSCIC 2014). At the end of the reporting period for 2014–15, there was an overall annual increase of 6.7 per cent in the number of people subject to the Act in England with an 8.3 per cent annual increase in detentions in this period (HSCIC 2015). In Wales, there was a 14 per cent increase on the previous year in formal admissions in 2014–15 (Welsh Government 2015).

At the same time as an increase in detention rates, NHS England data collection indicated that between 2010–11 and 2013–14 the number of available mental health NHS beds had decreased by almost 8 per cent (CQC 2015b). This has led to limited ability to access the necessary appropriate 'bed' for the patient who requires it, and examples of patients travelling out of their local area more than doubled between 2011–13 and 2014–15 (CQC 2015b). The Welsh Government Health Statistics reported a 4 per cent decrease in bed availability during 2013–14 (Welsh Government Health Statistics 2015).

Interestingly, research from the *National Confidential Inquiry into Suicide and Homicide by People with Mental Illness: Annual Report 2015: England, Northern Ireland, Scotland and Wales* reported that suicide rates were increased for patients placed far from home and for patients under crisis resolution and home treatment teams, which 'may reflect reduced availability of local in-patient beds, with increasing reliance on home treatment as an alternative to admission and on beds that are out of the local area'.

The Commission on Acute Adult Psychiatric Care (2015) reported that in August 2014, in-patient ward occupancy rates in England were averaging 101 per cent and in some wards running at 138 per cent, against recommendations by the Royal College of Psychiatrists (2011) that bed occupancy rates should be 85 per cent or less. In response to some of this, the revised Code details responsibilities for accessing appropriate beds for admission in line with s.140 and 'reception of patients in cases of special urgency' (para 14.77–14.86).

The Commission on Acute Adult Psychiatric Care (2015) also identified five main themes in relation to the 'bed crisis'. These are summarised here:

- The so-called bed, or admission, crisis is very significantly a problem of discharges and alternatives to admission and can only be addressed through changes in services and the management of the whole system.
- There is a spectrum of pressure and performance from demoralised staff, trapped in constant crisis management, to staff working purposefully to deliver high-quality care.
- Many patients feel disenfranchised and excluded – there is a need for greater engagement.
- A significant data and information shortfall exists, making it difficult to understand what is happening throughout the system.
- In many services, there is a need for greater staff support, training and motivation in order to improve care and services.

These issues form part of the reason for the reported stress in the statutory role of the AMHP, who has 'all the responsibility for coordinating the process but none of the decision latitude' (Hudson and Webber 2012).

As can be seen from the above list of AMHP tasks, these are wide ranging. Several AMHP duties under the MHA merit further consideration:

Section 13. Section 13(1) sets out the duty of local authorities if they

> have reason to think that an application for admission to hospital or a guardianship application may need to be made in respect of a patient within their area, they shall make arrangements for an AMHP to consider the patient's case on their behalf.

The AMHP must 'have regard to any wishes expressed by relatives of the patient or any other relevant circumstances' in decisions about making an application. If they conclude, having done so, that it is 'necessary or proper' to make an application, then they should do so (s.13(1A)).

Section 13(2) places a duty on AMHPs to interview patients in a suitable manner before making any application and to satisfy themselves that detention in a hospital is 'in all the circumstances of the case' the most appropriate way of a patient being provided with care and treatment. Interviewing in a suitable manner includes consideration of interpreters, British Sign Language and other signers, communication aids and cultural issues. AMHPs must also consider whether the assessment should be delayed, subject to considerations of risk, if the patient is under the influence of alcohol or drugs, or perhaps behind a closed door, and what to do if the patient is likely to be unhappy about the AMHP's presence in the patient's home to undertake the necessary assessment (Code ch. 14). Patients should usually be given the opportunity of seeing the AMHP alone during the assessment unless risks preclude this (Code 14.54), and if the patient wants someone else present, then ordinarily AMHPs should assist in securing that person's attendance (14.53). This could be a CC or family member, for example.

In *M v South West London & St George's Mental Health NHS Trust* [2008], the court held that there is no set time that must be taken in interviewing the patient and that s.13 allowed for some flexibility. If a patient refuses to talk with the AMHP, the AMHP should use his or her own professional expertise in coming to a conclusion as to whether an application is necessary, taking into consideration 'all the circumstances of the case' (s.13(2)).

AMHPs must also consider a patient's case if requested to do so by an NR (s.13(4)) and provide reasons in writing if they do not make an application.

The AMHP will need to identify relatives (s.26) and take their views into account (s.13). There are additional duties in relation to the NR (s.11) considered further in Chapter 7.

Finally, the Code recommends that the AMHP should liaise with others involved in the patient's care, such as the care coordinator, statutory or voluntary agencies (para 14.66–14.70). Where children are concerned, AMHPs should ensure that they have liaised with any necessary services and have access to information about care of children or any parenting issues that should inform their assessment. This may require the AMHP to have contact with the necessary child protection services, arranging joint visits and considering whether or not children should be present at the assessment and whether any other arrangements should be made for their care. There is additional guidance for AMHPs when assessing a young person (under 18) or a child (under 16) (Code ch.19). This includes identifying who has parental responsibility (PR) (s.3, Children Act 1989) and any child arrangement orders that may be in place (Code para 19.8). Children and young people may be under the Care Programme Approach, but as noted in Refocusing CPA (DH 2008), it is important for AMHPs to be aware of the broader pathway of care:

> CPA is not the only care planning method for children and young people and its use needs to be coordinated with the other systems e.g. CAF (Common Assessment Framework) and local systems for Looked After Children.

Section 11. This section refers to the AMHP's duties in relation to the NR. Identification of the NR, application to the court for the appointment of an acting NR and their powers and rights are all discussed in Chapter 7.

The role is a significant safeguard for the patient against arbitrary detention or community compulsion. The NR can object to an application for guardianship or s.3. They can order the discharge (s.23) of their relative from some sections and, although rarely used now, they can make applications for detention and guardianship. The law sets down the duties of the AMHP in relation to the NR as follows:

- s.11(3) To take such steps as are practicable to inform the nearest relative before or within a reasonable time after an application for the admission for a patient for assessment (s.2) that an application is being, or has been made and of their rights of discharge under s.23.
- s.11(4) An AMHP may not make an application for admission for treatment or a guardianship application in respect of a patient in either of the following cases:
  - (a) The nearest relative of the patient has notified that professional or the LSSA on whose behalf they are acting, that he objects to the application being made; or
  - (b) That professional has not consulted the person appearing to be the nearest relative unless it appears to the professional that in the circumstances such consultation is not reasonably practicable or would involve unreasonable delay.

Consultation within the meaning of s.11(4) requires 'the communication of a genuine invitation to give advice and genuine consideration of that advice' (*Briscoe (Habeas Corpus)* [1998]).

If, following such consultation, the NR 'objects' to an application for admission for treatment or a guardianship application, the AMHP cannot make the application. The NR need not use the word 'object' but the AMHP must clarify whether or not this is what they mean (*B v Cygnet Healthcare* [2008]). The NR could 'perhaps wish to sit on the fence' and avoid consultation (*R v Ealing LBC* [2002]) and may not, in fact, be objecting.

'Unreasonable delay' cannot be relied upon simply because the AMHP has left consultation to the 'very last moment' to avoid the NR (*GD v Edgware Community Hospital* [2008]) or has chosen not to consult at all due to other pressures (*GP v Derby City Council* [2012]) or because of a belief that the NR would not object if they had been consulted (*R v South London & Maudsley NHS Foundation Trust* [2010]).

The consultation process prior to s.3 or guardianship applications provides an opportunity for the NR to consider what should happen. As they have the power to object, this should be part of the consideration and not avoided by the AMHP. The AMHP need not decide whether the objection is reasonable or not, but if they remain clear that the NR is objecting and believe it is 'necessary or proper' to make an application, they cannot proceed without further recourse to county court.

However, the AMHP need not consult if this is 'not reasonably practicable' (s.11(4)(b)). This could be relied upon if, for example: the NR cannot be consulted due to illness or incapacity, is refusing to be consulted or is either un-contactable or details of their whereabouts are unknown after attempts have been made. If the NR is impossible to identify or contact, it may be possible to rely on 'impracticability' as long as the AMHP can record clearly the steps taken to attempt to consult.

In *R v Bristol* [2005] the court ruled that 'practicable' need not mean 'available' as the 1999 Code guidance stated. The word 'practicable' could be interpreted to take account of the patient's right to respect for their private and family life in Article 8 ECHR. Therefore, AMHPs could decide on an individual case basis whether it was 'practicable' to consult the NR, bearing in mind A8(1) and (2) ECHR. In the Bristol case, the patient had clearly indicated over a period of time that she did not wish her sister consulted as 'they did not get on' and had not seen each other for several years.

However, more recently, in *TW v Enfield* [2014] the Court of Appeal considered the Bristol case above alongside the guidance in the 2008 Code and considered that both were incomplete and therefore not to be relied upon.

> In summary, it seems to me that, as a matter of construction of section 11(4), when an [AMHP] is considering whether it is 'reasonably practicable' to consult the nearest relative before making an application to admit a … patient (for s.3) … the section imposes on the [AMHP] an obligation to strike a balance between the patient's Article 5 right not to be detained unless that is done by a procedure that is in accordance with the law and the patient's Article 8(1) right to her private life.

The issue of disclosure of confidential information as a result of consultation is not an easy one for AMHPs to negotiate. However, current guidance in the 2015 Code reflects the TW case above when it states at para 14.61 that should the AMHP consider that consultation would have a detrimental impact on the patient, such as emotional distress, deterioration in mental state, physical harm, financial or other exploitation as a result of the consultation process, he or she may rely on impracticability. However, the AMHP should respect the balancing act between the patient's right to respect for privacy (A8) alongside the patient's right to liberty (A5) and should record why consultation would not be justified and proportionate in the particular circumstances of the case.

The body of case law around the identification of and consultation with NRs gives an indication of how important a safeguard the role is considered to be by the courts. It is fair to say that this area of the MHA represents a significant litigation risk for AMHPs and LSSAs.

→ **KEY CASE ANALYSIS** ←

GP v Derby City Council [2012] EWHC 1451 (Admin) (2012) MHLO 58

This case demonstrated both the strict approach applied to a reliance on 'unreasonable delay' as a reason to not consult a NR and the gravity with which the courts view the s.11(4) requirement to consult:

GP applied for a writ of habeas corpus following detention under section 3 on the basis that the AMHP had not consulted with the NR as required by s.11(4) MHA. The patient was detained under section 2, which was due to expire at midnight on the day the AMHP conducted the assessment, in respect of an s.3 application. The AMHP made a number of unsuccessful attempts to telephone the NR and was under pressure from nursing staff to complete the application as it was claimed that the patient required transfer to a psychiatric intensive care unit and that this could only be done if the patient was detained under section 3.

The court held that the decision to dispense with the consultation was unlawful on the basis that: subsequent events did not show any urgency for transfer (this happened more than two weeks later); the assessment concluded at 4.30pm and therefore there would have been sufficient time for the AMHP to drive to the NR's address (a 30-minute journey).

In the course of the judgment, the judge made the following comment:

> [S]ection 11 provides constitutional protection for those that are faced with detention under the Mental Health Act. Compliance with the requirements of section 11(4) is therefore the price which is paid for the ability of those charged with the treatment of those with mental illnesses and disabilities to detain people without immediate recourse to a court and in a way which is compliant with Article 5. Thus there is a heavy duty on those who carry out these tasks to ensure that those statutory provisions are complied with.

There may be situations where the AMHP concludes that the NR is not a suitable person to act as such, and s.29 allows the AMHP to make an application to the county court for consideration of displacement of the NR.

Section 139: Protection for acts done in pursuance of the MHA. Although AMHPs are required to act independently, they act on behalf of an LSSA while undertaking these duties. This means that the LSSA is vicariously liable for the AMHP's actions if legal proceedings are issued.

Section 139 offers a measure of protection from civil or criminal proceedings for professionals undertaking duties under the MHA. Proceedings cannot be brought against a professional unless he or she is deemed to have acted in bad faith or without reasonable care.

> **PRACTICE FOCUS**
>
> Xavier is a 17-year-old who has been referred for an MHA assessment. He lives with his parents and younger sister and has become increasingly psychotic and agitated. CAMHS have been working closely with the family alongside Children Services, but it does now appear that Xavier requires further admission.
>
> - What should the AMHP take into consideration in discharging their duties in sections 11 and 13?

However, in *TTM v London Borough of Hackney* [2011], the court circumscribed the protection under s.139 in holding that an automatic right to compensation applied when the patient's ECHR rights (in this case Article 5) were engaged, even though the AMHP was not deemed to have acted in bad faith or without reasonable care.

| *On-the-spot question* | Why is the independence of the AMHP so important? |

The police and courts

The police and courts play a role in mental health services as well as more specifically within the MHA.

The police inevitably have contact with vulnerable persons in the course of their duties. In addition, the police are a key agency in Multi-Agency Public Protection Arrangements (MAPPAs) and Multi-Agency Risk Assessment Conferences (MARACs). MAPPAs are discussed in more detail in Chapter 5.

More specifically, police have powers to remove persons found in a public place who appear mentally disordered and in need of immediate care or control (s.136). They have the power to execute warrants obtained under s.135 and to convey (s.137) or retake (s.138, s.18) certain patients, using force where necessary (see Chapter 3 for details).

AMHPs may have to attend a magistrates' court when applying for s.135 warrants or a county court when making an application in relation to the NR (s.29).

Chapter 5 looks in detail at the role of the courts with mental disorder and offending, as well as court diversion.

The approved clinician (AC) and the responsible clinician (RC)

For initial detention, guardianship or CTOs, a doctor is required to examine the patient and make decisions regarding the presence of mental disorder and whether to recommend compulsion. However, once a patient is subject to compulsion, a doctor does not necessarily need to be in charge of the treatment and care of the patient. The 2007 amendments to the MHA replaced the role of 'responsible medical officer' (RMO) who would have been in charge of the treatment of certain categories of patient with the role of responsible clinician (RC) defined in s.34 as 'the approved clinician with overall responsibility for the patient's case'. The approved clinician (AC) is defined in s.145 as a person approved by the Secretary of State or the Welsh ministers to act as an approved clinician for the purposes of this Act.

As with the AMHP, the crucial change is that the role is now competency based rather than belonging to a particular profession. The following professions are eligible to take on the role with the necessary competence and approval:

- Registered medical practitioners
- First-level nurses whose field of practice is mental health or learning disabilities
- Registered occupational therapists
- Registered social workers
- Chartered psychologists

> These professionals will bring particular expertise from their different backgrounds and may be able to work to demonstrate the necessary competencies to carry out the AC role.
>
> (NIMHE 2008)

The role of AC was broadened out to allow for non-medics to be in charge of treatment, particularly where the predominant treatment was not medication. For example, in a unit specialising in work with people with personality disorders, it may be more appropriate for a clinical psychologist to be in charge of their treatment if the interventions are mainly based on psychological therapies. ACs can only carry out their role in relation to a treatment they are qualified to give. Non-medics, as in the example above, would be required to request a review of medication by an AC from the medical profession.

Although doctors will always provide the medical recommendations for initial use of compulsory powers, it is possible that a renewal of detention, for example, could take place without the involvement of any doctors. Concerns were raised (and rejected by the Government) during the passage of the 2007 MHA amendments through Parliament that this situation would not provide objective medical expertise to justify the detention (as discussed in Chapter 2). The issue is yet to be considered by the courts, perhaps due to the fact that the vast majority of ACs and RCs continue to be doctors. ACs and RCs are Public Authorities for the purposes of s.6 HRA 1998.

Main duties of the AC and RC

The AC's main functions refer to treatment issues and consent. They can prevent an informal patient from leaving the ward in certain circumstances (s.5(2)), may be required to write reports for Mental Health Tribunals or court reports for patients subject to criminal proceedings. They may visit and examine a patient at the request of an NR in certain circumstances (s.24). Responsible clinicians will be ACs with the 'most appropriate expertise to meet the patient's main assessment and treatment needs' (Code 36.3).

The RC has specific statutory duties, including these:

- Overall responsibility for the patient's care (for those on certain sections of the Act)
- Reviewing progress, including assessing whether the patient still meets the legal criteria under the Act and discharging if he or she does not
- Granting leave (s.17)
- Considering an order from an NR to discharge the patient and blocking this if grounds are met (s.25)
- Renewing detention if grounds are met (s.20)
- Also, a range of duties and powers in relation to CTOs, including whether to make a CTO, the specifying condition, recalling a patient or revoking the CTO, and decisions on extending or discharging from a CTO (ss.17A–17G and s.20A)

Approval to work as an approved clinician and a responsible clinician

The competency requirements of an AC require the potential approving body to be satisfied that it is able to demonstrate the relevant competencies, which include an applied knowledge of law and policy, assessment skills in identifying mental disorder and the range of appropriate treatments,

ability-to-care plan, ability to provide effective leadership to a multidisciplinary team and being up to date with equality and cultural diversity issues.
Evidence of these competencies could be by way of a portfolio.

Approval as an AC automatically gives doctors approval to provide
medical recommendations for compulsion under the MHA (s.12 MHA).
However, not all s.12 doctors will be approved to be an AC because the
processes for s.12 and AC approval differ, and ACs have additional powers within the Act, as listed above.

An approving authority may only approve a person to be an AC where
he or she fulfils one of the professional requirements listed above, is able
to demonstrate relevant competencies and within the last two years has
completed an initial AC training course. Approval runs for five years.

On-the-spot questions

What are the ECHR issues for a non-medically
trained RC when considering a renewal of detention?
When do you think a non-medic AC might be more
appropriate?

The independent mental health advocate (IMHA)

S.130A places a duty on the Secretary of State and the Welsh ministers
to arrange for IMHA services to be available for patients who 'qualify'.
The IMHA should not be confused with the independent mental capacity
advocate (IMCA) in the Mental Capacity Act 2005 (MCA). As we have
seen, the MHA can apply to people regardless of their capacity to consent, and the 'qualifying' requirements are about which section of the
MHA applies rather than about capacity. With the introduction of specific statutory advocacy services within the Care Act 2014 and Social Services Wellbeing (Wales) Act 2014, it is possible that some patients may
have more than one advocate involved in their care for differing reasons.

The IMHA may come from a social work or other professional
background.

The Code of Practice describes the IMHA role as

> an additional safeguard for patients who are subject to the Act.
> IMHAs are specialist advocates who are trained specifically to work
> within the framework of the Act and enable patients to participate
> in decision-making.

(para 6.3)

Training and competencies of an IMHA

Regulations set out that IMHAs may only act as such if they

- have appropriate experience or training or an appropriate combination of experience and training
- are persons of integrity and good character
- are able to act independently of any person who is professionally concerned with the qualifying patient's medical treatment
- are able to act independently of any person who requests that person to visit or interview the qualifying patient (MHA 1983 [Independent Mental Health Advocates (England) Regulations 2008])

The Department of Health has issued guidance on what would constitute appropriate experience and training. The IMHA Society (England) is currently campaigning for national reform of the IMHA service in relation to producing national standardised frameworks for training and delivering services (see Further reading list below).

Duties of an IMHA

The main duties of the IMHA are to assist in helping patients obtain information about and understanding of

- their rights under the Act;
- the rights which other people (e.g. NRs) have in relation to them under the Act;
- the particular parts of the Act which apply to them (e.g. the basis on which they are detained) and which therefore make them eligible for advocacy;
- any conditions or restrictions to which they are subject (e.g. as a condition of leave of absence from hospital, as a condition of a community treatment order, or as a condition of conditional discharge);
- any medical treatment that they are receiving or might be given
- the reasons for that treatment (or proposed treatment); and
- the legal authority for providing that treatment, and the safeguards and other requirements of the Act that would apply to that treatment (para 6.12 Code).

IMHAs are entitled to visit and interview patients privately, as well as interview any professional concerned with the patient's medical treatment. They should be able to access and inspect records relating to the patient's detention and treatment and any aftercare arrangements under s.117.

The role is titled 'independent' mental health advocate. S.130A(4) states:

> In making arrangements under this section, the appropriate national authority shall have regard to the principle that any help available to a patient under the arrangements should, so far as practicable, be provided by a person who is independent of any person who is professionally concerned with the patients medical treatment.

The independence of the role should provide a significant safeguard for patients. The serious case review of Winterbourne View (Flynn and Citarella 2012) noted that of 48 patients, 41 were detained. However, patients 'were without voice or representation', and access to advocacy services was controlled by staff.

The Health Committee post-legislative scrutiny of the MHA 2007 recognised that the introduction of IMHAs was a significant improvement to the legislation. However, it also recommended that the IMHA service become an 'opt-out' rather than 'opt-in' service. This was as a result of some reported difficulties, both in patients being given their rights to access an IMHA but also because of variation in the ability to provide prompt services. The Health Committee also reported that there was a 'compelling case to extend advocacy provision' to the informal patients. Wales has extended its provision of IMHA services accordingly, and the Mental Health (Independent Advocacy) (England) Bill 2015–16 also proposes extending IMHA provisions.

On-the-spot questions

How might a detained patient benefit from the involvement of an IMHA?
What are the arguments for extending IMHA provisions to patients who are not detained?
Why is there a need for IMHA services when there are already IMCA services established?

Further reading

Books

Allen, R. (2014) *The Role of the Social Worker in Adult Mental Health Services*. Looks at how social work can be involved in improving adult mental health services and achieve better outcomes for families and service users. It emphasises the importance of social work within mental health, particularly at a time of organisational change.

Brown, R. (2013) *The Approved Mental Health Professional's Guide to Mental Health Law.* Practice focused and providing detail on the law, in particular on the duties and powers of the AMHP.

Department of Health (2004) *The Ten Essential Shared Capabilities – A Framework for the Whole of the Mental Health Workforce.* The essential shared capabilities (ESCs) are complementary to other occupational standards and frameworks. Although this document refers to mental health education and training in England, the capabilities listed are relevant to all those working in mental health services, whether professionally qualified or not.

Websites

www.imhasociety.org. This English-based website has helpful information about the role of the IMHA as well as links with advocacy in the Care Act 2014.

www.bihr.org.uk. *Mental Health Advocacy and Human Rights: Your Guide.* This short guide, co-produced by the British Institute of Human Rights and various voluntary- and community-sector organisations in England, is very practical and easy to read, providing information on advocacy and human rights as they apply in mental health. It includes helpful links for human rights and the MCA, MHA and DoLS.

2
MENTAL DISORDER

AT A GLANCE THIS CHAPTER COVERS:

- current legal definition of mental disorder and compatibility with European Convention on Human Rights
- exclusions from the definition of mental disorder
- mental disorder, children and young people
- mental disorder and learning disabilities
- ethics, models and terminology
- links with capacity

Current legal definition of mental disorder and compatibility with the European Convention on Human Rights

> No freeman ought to be taken or imprisoned or disseized of his freehold, liberties or privileges, or outlawed, or exiled, or in any manner destroyed, or deprived of his life, liberty or property but by judgement of his peers, or by the law of the land.
>
> (Magna Carta of 1215)

Moving forward more than seven hundred years, Article 5(1) of the European Convention on Human Rights (ECHR) similarly states:

> Everyone has the right to liberty and security of person. No-one shall be deprived of his liberty save in the following cases and in accordance with a procedure prescribed by law.

One of the exceptions is

> the lawful detention of persons of unsound mind.
>
> (Art 5(1)(e))

The right to liberty is therefore a limited rather than an absolute human right, and unsoundness of mind may provide lawful justification for the detention of an individual.

Our domestic procedure for lawfully depriving someone of liberty due to unsoundness of mind is the MHA. The deprivation of liberty of adults who lack capacity may also be authorised under DoLS or by the Court of Protection (see Chapter 8).

The language of A5 ECHR is closely reflected in the legal criteria for detention in the MHA.

Unsoundness of mind is not further defined in the Convention; however, a series of ECHR cases – the most widely cited being the Winterwerp case – have identified the following essential requirements for a person to be legally of unsound mind:

- The individual must be reliably shown, by objective medical expertise, to be of unsound mind, unless emergency detention is required.
- The individual's mental disorder must be of a kind to warrant compulsory confinement. The deprivation of liberty must be shown to have been necessary in the circumstances.
- The mental disorder, verified by objective medical evidence, must persist throughout the period of detention.

Winterwerp v Netherlands [1979] EHRR 387

Mr Winterwerp was detained in hospital initially on an emergency basis, and his detention was subsequently renewed for a number of years on the basis of applications to the court by his wife and then latterly by the public prosecutor. Mr Winterwerp made several written requests to be discharged in the course of his detention. His primary application to the ECtHR was that he did not have a mental disorder and that he had not been adequately examined by doctors in the course of his detention and that this was in breach of Article 5(1). This ground of appeal was unsuccessful, but the case has become important because of the court's consideration of what constitutes 'unsound mind': the court found that no one could be detained as a 'person of unsound mind' in the absence of objective medical expertise establishing that his or her mental state is such as to justify his compulsory hospitalisation. Anything else would be arbitrary and incompatible with A5. Furthermore, the mental disorder must be of a kind or degree warranting compulsory confinement.

Continued detention requires persistence of the disorder. This is more an issue for those who renew or review detentions in hospital rather than the initial decision-makers.

On-the-spot question	Apart from unsoundness of mind, can you think of any other circumstances where the deprivation of a person's liberty would not be a breach of his or her right to liberty, as in A5 ECHR?

The definition of mental disorder is to be found in section 1, MHA. The MHA can only apply to those who are deemed to be mentally disordered; therefore, this becomes the first of several gateways before the powers within the MHA can be used. In simple terms, if a person does not have a mental disorder as defined in s.1, then the rest of the MHA does not apply to them.

Mental disorder is defined in s.1(1) as 'any disorder or disability of the mind'. This definition was a consequence of the 2007 amendments to the MHA. As we have seen, prior to the amendments, mental disorder was subdivided into categories of mental illness, mental impairment, psychopathic disorder and severe mental impairment. The Government's stated aim was to simplify the definition and to focus on needs and risks rather than labels.

The Code of Practice (ch. 25) provides a non-exhaustive list of examples of 'clinically recognised conditions' falling within the s.1 definition, as follows:

- Affective disorders, such as depression and bipolar disorder
- Schizophrenia and delusional disorders
- Neurotic, stress-related and somatoform disorders, such as anxiety, phobic disorders, obsessive compulsive disorders, post-traumatic stress disorder and hypochondriacal disorders
- Organic mental disorders such as dementia and delirium (however caused)
- Personality and behavioural changes caused by brain injury or damage (however acquired)
- Personality disorders
- Mental and behavioural disorders caused by psychoactive substance use
- Eating disorders, non-organic sleep disorders and non-organic sexual disorders
- Learning disabilities
- Autistic spectrum disorders (including Asperger's syndrome)
- Behavioural and emotional disorders of children and young people

These lists are based on the manuals used in psychiatry to identify and treat mental illnesses: the *International Classification of Diseases (ICD)* and the *Diagnostic and Statistical Manual (DSM)*. Generally, the *ICD* (edition 10) is used in the United Kingdom and the *DSM* (edition V) is used in the United States. The manuals use different language and are not consistent in what conditions are included, although there is an increasing body of academic opinion that the manuals should be harmonised in the interests of cross-border understanding and consistency of clinical research.

It may be surprising to some that issues such as eating disorders, personality disorders, spirit possession, some childhood disorders, learning disabilities and autistic spectrum conditions are all within the list of possible mental disorders coming within the scope of s.1 MHA.

These manuals, subject to some controversy over the years, provide a set of definitions and symptoms to assist with research, diagnosis and treatment of the conditions listed within them. However, for the purposes of s.1, mental disorder could include disorders not yet within the manual. Equally, the courts have held that the presence of a clinical diagnosis based on the *DSM* will not, in itself, necessarily confirm the presence of mental disorder for legal purposes (*DL-H v Devon Partnership NHS Trust* [2010]).

These manuals are firmly based on a medical model of understanding and responding to mental distress.

ICD codes are used in research and practice. They provide a 'global health information standard' used to 'manage healthcare, monitor outcomes and allocate resources' (WHO 2015). There is an expectation generally in mental health that psychiatry will provide a diagnostic label to the individual once this person has been assessed. Labels can, of course, be helpful, for example, to access appropriate services or as a useful shorthand in professional communication, but in the field of psychiatry, they have their limitations and, of course, can be stigmatising.

Psychiatry is not an exact science and what constitutes a disorder or disability of the mind is constantly evolving and subject to the views of society as well as prevailing cultural norms. One extraordinary historical example of this would be the diagnosis of 'Drapetomania', created by a doctor in nineteenth-century America; this purported mental disorder concerned black slaves who ran away from their owners for no apparent reason.

Mental health law provides a term that deals with 'disorder' but does not define mental health. Disorder is diagnosed and treated by medical experts. This further embeds the term in a medical model of thinking. However, it remains difficult to provide an exact and absolute definition of mental disorder.

In the Winterwerp case, the court stated that a definition of 'unsound mind' was

> not one that can be given a definitive interpretation … it is a term whose meaning is constantly evolving as research in psychiatry progresses, an increasing flexibility in treatment is developing and society's attitude to mental illness changes, in particular so that a greater understanding of the problems of mental patients is becoming wide-spread.

Given that this case is from 1979, one may wish to consider what has changed since then in terms of what would and would not be considered a mental disorder. Some examples of changes to the manuals are listed here:

- Homosexuality was finally removed from the *DSM* in 1986 and from the *ICD* in 1992.
- Hoarding disorder was added to the *DSM* in 2013 but is not yet in the *ICD*.

Having seen the wide definition for what could be included as a mental disorder for the purposes of the MHA, it is important to note what conditions are excluded from the s.1 definition, or where a condition's inclusion is circumscribed:

Exclusions from the definition of mental disorder

Dependence on drugs or alcohol is explicitly excluded from the definition of mental disorder:

> s.1(3) Dependence on alcohol or drugs is not considered to be a disorder or disability of the mind.

This means that dependence alone is not to be considered a mental disorder within s.1. However, the interaction of drug or alcohol dependence with mental disorder is complex, and any conditions arising from drug or alcohol use, such as drug-induced psychosis or Korsakoff's syndrome, could be within the s.1 definition.

This exclusion raises some ethical questions. On the one hand, the fact that someone is dependent on drugs or alcohol should not, by itself, mean he or she is pathologised as mentally disordered. On the other hand, members of this group are presumably deemed to be responsible for their actions in a way that those with mental disorders may not be. The Equality Act 2010 does not include substance or alcohol dependence in its protected characteristics, whereas a mental health condition may fall within the definition of disability, thereby triggering statutory protection under the Act.

The Government view during debate about the 2007 MHA amendments was that these were social and behavioural problems 'manifested in varying degrees of habit and dependency' (Government, Cmnd 7320, cited in Jones 2015).

However, there remains a close relationship between misuse of drugs and alcohol and mental health problems. It may be difficult to disentangle use and dependency from depression and anxiety or psychosis. The ongoing circular debate between services about whether the substance or alcohol misuse causes the mental health problem, or vice versa, has not provided any solutions. It has led to battles over which services are the most appropriate to meet the primary needs of the client and, indeed, what the primary needs are. It is possible that all problems are seen to stem from substance or alcohol misuse, and the diagnosis of significant mental or physical health problems is lost within this assumption. Alternatively, those with significant mental health problems may not be provided with adequate therapies or treatment for significant substance misuse problems because the mental health problem is seen as the central issue. A study from 2002 noted that 44 per cent of London community mental health team patients had problem drug use within the previous year, while 75 per cent of drug service users and 85 per cent of alcohol service users had experienced a psychiatric disorder within the previous year. Inner-city areas reported a likely higher prevalence (*British Journal of Psychiatry* 2003).

Research also indicates that those with a mental disorder who also misuse substances present a higher risk of violence, which can feed into public perceptions of madness and dangerousness, although those who misuse substances and do not have a mental disorder are already considered a high-risk group in relation to violence (University of Manchester 2015).

On-the-spot question   In what circumstances might someone with dependence on drugs or alcohol fall within the definition of mental disorder?

Mental disorder, children and young people

As stated, the MHA does not have a lower age limit, except for one section dealing with guardianship orders. Therefore, it is possible for the Act to apply to children and adolescents if they have a mental disorder and other relevant criteria are met. The MHA Code refers to those under 16 as children and those aged 16–17 years as young people (ch. 19).

It is, of course, unlikely that the MHA would be the first intervention to be considered for most children or young people. Many children have developmental disorders that are considered part of maturation, and use of the MHA would not necessarily be considered appropriate. Alternatives should be considered, which might include the possibility of referral and input from Children and Adolescent Mental Health Services (CAMHS). For a small group of children or young people, an informal admission to psychiatric hospital may have to be considered. Other routes may include decision-making by parents or others with parental responsibility; or use of other statutory powers under, for example, The Children Act 1989. A smaller group of children and young people may, however, find themselves subject to compulsion under the MHA.

The Health and Social Care Information Centre (HSCIC) publishes annual statistics on the use of the MHA. Some of the worrying aspects of statistics from 2013–14 showed that under 18s were spending time as detained patients on adult wards due to a lack of specialist units being available. There have been difficulties in accessing specialist adolescent and children services for those in need of admission and detention, and adult wards then become the only option in emergency situations.

In addition, a significant number of children have been detained in police custody following the use of police powers to remove a mentally disordered person to a 'place of safety' (see Chapter 3). In 2012–13, 263 children were held in police cells following the use of this power and in 2013–14 the number was 236 (HSCIC 2014).

Theoretically, a child, no matter how young, could be subject to detention and treatment under the MHA. However, both the Act itself and the Code of Practice provide some additional safeguards.

Section 131A states that where psychiatric hospital admission is required for under 18s, the managers of the hospital must ensure that the environment is suitable having regard to their age. In doing this, they should consult someone who has knowledge or experience of under-18s admissions.

In addition the Code offers guidance on those arranging an assessment under the MHA:

> As part of their role in setting up an assessment AMHPs should consider whether to inform the relevant local authority children's services that an assessment is being arranged and request that any relevant information about the child or young person is provided prior to the assessment. The AMHP should consider

with children's services whether a representative from children's services should attend the assessment.

and

at least one of the people involved in assessing whether a child or young person should be admitted to hospital, and if so whether they should be detained under the Act ... should be a CAMHS professional.

(ch. 19)

The Code also makes it clear that children and young people who require admission should remain as near to their families and communities as possible.

On-the-spot questions

What are the implications of having no lower age limit for mental disorder?
What issues do you think should be considered in providing a suitable psychiatric hospital environmental for a child or adolescent?

Mental disorder and learning disabilities

Learning disability is defined in the Mental Health Act as

a state of arrested or incomplete development of the mind which includes significant impairment of intelligence and social functioning.

(s.1(4))

A great deal of debate has taken place as to whether people with learning disabilities should be grouped together with people with mental illnesses, personality disorders and other mental disorders.

Campaigners in favour of removing learning disability as a category of patient subject to the MHA included Mencap, which argued that learning disability was neither an illness nor something that statutory interventions within the MHA should cover.

As the amendments to the MHA were debated, Lord Rix made the following point in the House of Commons:

a learning disability is completely different from a mental illness, and should not be treated as such.

(Hansard 2007)

Why, then, were learning disabilities and mental illness grouped together in this legislation?

There was an acceptance within the debate that someone with a learning disability could also experience a separate mental disorder requiring intervention under the MHA. Indeed, research suggests that those with learning disabilities are significantly more likely to experience some mental disorders. Research collated by Estia concluded that those with learning disabilities were three times more likely to suffer from schizophrenia, have higher rates of bipolar disorder and be vulnerable to depression and generalised anxiety disorders; and for those with Down's Syndrome, a higher prevalence of dementia, at 55 per cent of those over the age of 60–69 years (Turning Point and Estia Centre 2006).

Alongside this is a concern that those with a learning disability may be subject to diagnostic overshadowing; that is, everything is deemed to be as a result of the learning disability, and physical or mental health problems are not diagnosed, because of communication difficulties or other issues and assumptions about learning disability. These assumptions can stand in the way of appropriate treatment (Mencap 2007).

However, learning disability was retained within the MHA, along with additional conditions that had to be met if the longer-term sections of the Act were to apply on the basis purely of the learning disability rather than any concurrent mental disorder. These conditions are within section 1(2A), which provides that, for certain sections, such as section 3 (admission for treatment) or section 7 (guardianship), the learning disability has to be associated with

> abnormally aggressive or seriously irresponsible conduct on his part.

The Code provides further guidance:

> Neither term is defined in the Act, and it is not possible to state with any precision exactly what type of conduct could be considered to fall into either category. It will, inevitably, depend not only on the nature of the behaviour and the circumstances in which it is exhibited, but also on the extent to which that conduct gives rise to a serious risk to the health or safety of the patient or the health or safety of other people, or both.
>
> (Code ch. 20.9)

The Code makes it clear that assumptions about presentation should not be made. A full assessment by a range of professionals, including a specialist learning disability psychiatrist and psychologist, with the involvement of families, should be made. There was, again, much debate about these additional requirements. The Hansard debate shows Lord Rix arguing against the additional requirements:

> Aggression and irresponsibility may be symptomatic of physical health problems, or stress. Allowing people with a learning disability who are aggressive or irresponsible to be sectioned on that basis may lead to physical health problems being missed.

He goes on to say that it may 'allow the symptoms to overshadow the causes'.

The conduct can be historical rather than current. The courts have applied a high threshold to what constitutes seriously irresponsible conduct. For example:

- A wish by a 17-year-old to return to an inadequate family home where she had experienced neglect and possible sexual exploitation was not seriously irresponsible conduct (*Re F (Mental Health Act: Guardianship)* [2000]).
- A lack of road sense and tendency to rush into the road was not seriously irresponsible conduct (*London Borough of Newham v BS* [2003]).

  However, such cases are fact specific and therefore:

- A compulsion to pick up litter even from the road was held to be seriously irresponsible conduct (*R(GC) v Managers of the Kingswood Centre* [2008]).

With these qualifications, learning disability remains within the definition of mental disorder for the purposes of the MHA. It is therefore the responsibility of the clinician and the assessing team to ensure that a holistic assessment does not miss physical health problems. Those with learning disabilities should not be detained or held in hospital accommodation for longer than is necessary to provide treatment or assessment of the particular mental disorder.

The debate regarding the detention and treatment of people with learning disabilities was reignited following the 2011 *Panorama* exposé of systematic abuse, torture and criminal acts at the Winterbourne View Hospital, a specialist hospital for people with learning disabilities and challenging behaviours. The profoundly shocking video evidence gathered by the documentary makers led to closure of the hospital and the conviction of 11 care workers, 6 of whom received custodial sentences, and the case prompted a high level of media attention and a rapid response from the Government.

In *Transforming Care – a National Response to Winterbourne View Hospital* (DH 2012b), the Government set a target for those people with learning disabilities, inappropriately placed in hospital, to be moved to community care settings by June 2014. They went on to state that

> as a consequence, there will be a dramatic reduction in hospital placements for this group of people and the closure of large hospitals.

This target was entirely missed, and 2014–15 data showed that 2600 people with learning disabilities remained in hospital settings (HSCIC). A number of commissioned reports and policy documents seeking to address the failure have followed, most recently *Transforming Care for People with Learning Disabilities – Next Steps* (ADASS et al. 2015).

So, in terms of the initial gateway for use of the MHA, we have the wide definition of mental disorder; age limitations for guardianship; the exclusion of dependence on alcohol or drugs; additional requirements for some sections as they may apply to people with learning disabilities; and additional guidance and requirements in relation to the detention of children.

Ethics, models and terminology

As we have seen, the concept of mental disorder is complex, and we can see from the development of the law in this area that questions of the nature (or existence) of mental disorder, such as when the State should intervene, the use of compulsion, and the interaction with the criminal justice system, have developed and fluctuated in response to societal changes, clinical research and developments in treatments for mental disorder.

> People's understanding of how the mind works, together with their views on mental capacity, free will, determinism and social responsibility, combine to influence how they think the law should operate in this field.
>
> (Brown 2009)

The medical model and psychiatry remains the dominant discourse in mental health (Rogers and Pilgrim 2005). However, in modern mental health services, it is likely that there is more of a crossover between models with an increasing emphasis on the importance of listening to the service users' own perspective, regardless of models used. Service users value 'dignity, engagement, trust and regaining hope' above any individual model (*Open Mind Magazine* 2004). That said, it is important to have an understanding of models of mental disorder and the interventions each model promotes. This can be a helpful means for critically evaluating which models dominate law and practice.

Anti-psychiatry movements of the 1960s and 1970s argued that mental illness was a construct of social control. Tomas Szasz argued that mental illness simply did not exist, but was a form of moral control by the State and bourgeois/upper classes, and R. D. Laing argued that insanity was a perfectly sane response to an insane world.

The controlling aspects of mental health legislation, including detention of those who were perceived as mentally disordered, was seen as coercive and oppressive rather than helpful. Some civil libertarian perspectives would say that people should be free to make their own decisions about treatment and care and that the State should only intervene and use coercive powers over someone if a crime is committed, or perhaps where capacity is lost.

Alternatively, more welfarist approaches can tend to opt for intervention on behalf of someone if they cannot apparently manage or control the consequences of their behaviour. Welfarist approaches accept the concept of mental disorder and the need to intervene in some circumstances whether or not the individual would welcome this. It is a paternalistic approach whereby the State knows best irrespective of the individual's wishes and preferences.

Various approaches offer different explanations for the concept of mental disorder and models of understanding such as social or bio-psycho-social models may be important; however, the medical model of understanding has continued to provide the most significant influence on mental health law.

The doctor as the expert identifies the disorder or illness through diagnosis and identification of symptoms, then provides treatments that either cure and/or alleviate symptoms of the disorder. Critics of the dominance of this role argue that a purist psychiatric model rarely understands cultural perspectives or variations from a 'norm' set by the dominant culture in society and is therefore subject to bias and Eurocentric views. Service users might argue that the medical model pays insufficient attention to their personal autonomy:

> People have the right to define their own experiences for themselves and it is rarely helpful, more likely to be alienating for the clinician to insist that their understanding is correct.
> (Perkins and Repper, cited in Adams, Dominelli and Payne 2002)

However, many psychiatrists would argue that they have integrated an understanding of social and cultural perspectives into their work and take account of the whole person in their assessments and treatments.

One of the other crucial factors within the debate on mental disorder and psychiatry is the continued over-representation of certain groups within mental health services, particularly in the use of the Mental Health Act. Statistics for 2013–14 on the use of the MHA in England make it clear that 85 per cent of the population in England are white but make up 72 per cent of the detained population. However, black or black British make up 3.5 per cent of the English population as a whole but 10 per cent of the detained population. The apparent over-representation is even starker when looking at compulsion in the community, with 66 per cent of those subject to a CTO being white and 17 per cent being black or black British (HSCIC 2014). In 2014–15, 37.5 per cent of white in-patients were detained, whereas 56.9 per cent of black or black British patients were detained (HSCIC 2015).

Government policy revisits this issue regularly. For example, in *No Health Without Mental Health* (2011), they reiterate that 'some black groups have admission rates around three times higher than average … migrant groups and their children are at two to eight times greater risk of psychosis. African-Caribbean people are particularly likely to be subject to compulsory treatment under the MHA and South East Asian women are apparently less likely to receive timely, appropriate mental health services, even for severe mental health conditions.'

There is a wealth of research which substantiates that admission rates for black groups have actually increased, with black patients being more likely to be assessed as unable to consent to treatment, held in more secure settings and kept in hospital for longer periods of time than their white counterparts. There is no agreement over the reasons for this over-representation and there are some fierce debates about the contribution of institutional racism.

Psychiatrists Singh and Burns (2006) challenge the concept of 'institutionalised racism' as an explanation for the above, reporting that this leads to

> a self fulfilling prophecy by contributing to mistrust of services by ethnic minorities thereby leading to delayed help seeking with increased use of detention and coercive treatments for ethnic minority patients.

However, Suman Fernando points to continued institutional racism, flawed research and a Eurocentric value base contributing to the problem (Fernando 2010).

The Mental Health Act Commission also responded to the Singh and Burns paper:

> At root, this position seems to be concerned to protect psychiatry as a science (and sometimes psychiatrists as individuals) from the suspicions of cultural bias or 'racism'.

and

> our position is simply that the proportion of people from Black and minority ethnic groups admitted to and detained in mental health services is much higher than we would expect; and that the reason for this should be looked for within the spectrum of possibilities between the extreme positions that there is either an epidemic of mental illness amongst certain black groups, or that such groups are corralled into detention without proper clinical cause. We doubt that either of these extreme positions holds the answer and do not believe that setting them up as a straw-man, debating positions is helpful.
>
> (MHAC 12th Biennial Report 2008)

This is a complex and likely multifactorial issue; however, it is incumbent on professionals exercising functions under the MHA to have due regard to the risk of inaccurate assumptions or prejudices tainting the assessment process:

> Difference should not be confused with disorder. No-one may be considered to be mentally disordered solely because of their political, religious or cultural beliefs, values or opinions, unless there are proper clinical grounds to believe that there are symptoms or manifestations of a disability or disorder of the mind.
>
> (para 3.6)

The ECHR has highlighted the same point. In the Winterwerp case, the judgment includes a discussion of the nature of unsoundness of mind and concludes that the detention of a person on the basis of unsoundness of mind

> obviously cannot be taken as permitting the detention of a person simply because his views or behaviour deviate from the norms prevailing in a particular society.

On-the-spot questions How should services respond to the fact that the black population is over-represented within the MHA?
How has the concept of risk and public protection influenced the amendments to the MHA?

Links with capacity

Compulsion is not possible under the MCA in respect of persons with capacity to make decisions. However, compulsion is possible under the MHA. The MHA is the only law that allows for the detention (deprivation of liberty) and treatment of mental disorder against the will of someone with capacity to refuse. For this reason, issues of human rights, less restrictive alternatives and a balance to the medical model all become of utmost importance.

PRACTICE FOCUS

Ashkir

Ashkir is a 23-year-old Somalian man who came to the United Kingdom as an asylum seeker four years ago. Most of Ashkir's family were killed in Somalia, but his brother, aged 21, lives with him in a bedsit.

The police removed Ashkir under s.136 MHA to a place of safety this evening because he was waving a pole at passers-by while dancing naked. When members of the public attempted to talk to him, he shouted and seemed agitated and unpredictable.

At the place of safety, Ashkir must be examined by a doctor as soon as possible. If the doctor concludes that Ashkir has a mental disorder, an AMHP must also interview him and consider the views and wishes of any relatives and others caring for him as well as Ashkir's views. The AMHP must take all relevant circumstances into account, including his housing, employment, cultural and social circumstances and finances. One of the circumstances that the doctor and AMHP have to consider is Ashkir's self-reported use of illicit substances prior to being seen by police.

- What are the exclusions in section 1 and how might they apply here?
- On what basis might the doctor conclude that Ashkir may have a mental disorder in need of further assessment?

Further reading

Books

Gilbert, P. (2010) *The Value of Everything: Social Work and Its Importance in the Field of Mental Health*. An overview of the development of mental health law and policy and the role of social work in mental health services.

Rogers, A. and D. Pilgrim (2006) *A Sociology of Mental Health and Illness*. This book offers a critical analysis of psychiatry and models of mental disorder.

Websites

www.blackmentalhealth.org.uk. A website providing news, briefings and reports and campaigns on the subject of black mental health in the United Kingdom.

www.bihr.org.uk. The British Institute of Human Rights – this is a helpful website with easy-to-read free resources. Helpful for service users as well as social workers.

www.drugscope.blogspot.co.uk. Although DrugScope went into liquidation in 2015, the website has retained many reports and information on drug use that are essential for those working in health and social services.

www.slam.nhs.uk. Estia Centre. This is a 'training, research and development resource for people who support adults with intellectual disabilities and additional mental health needs'. Estia has various publications on this topic, some of which are free. The centre is part of South London & Maudsley NHS Foundation Trust, London, and can be accessed at slam.nhs.uk.

3

CIVIL ADMISSIONS AND POLICE POWERS

AT A GLANCE THIS CHAPTER COVERS:

- civil admissions under Part II of the MHA
- police powers

There are various routes into hospital for assessment or treatment of mental disorder. Chapter 5 covers routes into or out of hospital via the courts or prison. This chapter looks in more detail at Part II of the Act (generally termed 'civil admissions') as well as the role of the police in admissions to a 'place of safety'. The chapter will look at the process for admission under those sections, the duties and powers of the AMHP, doctors and police. An overview of these sections, timescales, treatment rules, access to Tribunals and powers of the nearest relative is set out in grids throughout this chapter.

Civil admissions under Part II of the MHA

As we have seen, assessing professionals are required to consider the least restrictive option and maximise independence (Code para 1.2-1.6). They should attempt to avoid depriving someone of liberty wherever possible, considering whether alternatives such as community resources can be mobilised. This could, for example, include the use of crisis and home treatment teams whose general aim is to offer rapid assessment in a mental health crisis and, if possible, offer intensive treatment at home as an alternative to admission. If admission to hospital is necessary, they should consider use of informal admission under s.131 MHA or, where it is applicable, the use of the MCA 2005.

Section 2 – admission for assessment

Section 2 provides for patients to be admitted for assessment (or assessment followed by medical treatment) of a mental disorder for up to 28 days if grounds below are met. As can be seen from the grid, s.2 admissions are not 'renewable', and therefore the assessment should be completed within the 28-day period. Patients subject to s.2 are covered by Part IV consent to treatment provisions.

Part of the assessment may be to identify whether admission under s.3 is appropriate (*R v Wilson* [1996]). A further period of detention may be unnecessary if the patient responds to treatment and can be discharged or remain informally. No initial diagnosis is required in order to use s.2, and it may be that the assessment concludes that there is no mental disorder, even though this appeared to be the case on admission.

Table 3.1: Civil Admissions – Summary

Section	Duration	Consent to Treatment Provisions Apply (Part IV)?	Access to Mental Health Tribunal?	Nearest Relative Powers
2 – admission for assessment	Up to 28 days – not renewable	Yes	Patient can apply within first 14 days of detention No automatic hearing if they do not apply	To make an application for admission for assessment To order discharge from detention giving 72 hours' notice to hospital managers (s.23)
3 – admission for treatment	Up to six months, renewable for further six months, then annually	Yes	Patient can apply once during the six months from day of admission, then once in every period of renewal. Automatic reference for an MHT six months from admission if patient has not applied and then at three-year intervals	To make an application for admission for treatment To object to the application for section 3 To order discharge from detention giving 72 hours' notice to hospital managers
4 – emergency admission for assessment	Up to 72 hours Can be 'converted' to s.2 with the second medical recommendation	No	Notionally, patient could apply during the 72-hour period – the appeal would only proceed in the event that the s.4 is converted to an s.2.	To make an application for admission for assessment in an emergency To make an order to discharge from detention giving 72 hours' notice to hospital managers – section 23 as above

Grounds. The legal grounds for admission under section 2:

> S.2(2) An application for admission for assessment may be made in respect of a patient on the grounds that
>
> (a) he is suffering from mental disorder of a nature or degree which warrants the detention of the patient in a hospital for assessment (or for assessment followed by medical treatment) for at least a limited period; and
>
> (b) he ought to be so detained in the interests of his own health or safety or with a view to the protection of other persons.

Procedure. Use of sections 2 or 3 requires assessment by two medical practitioners and an AMHP. The medical practitioners make recommendations for admission to hospital, and the AMHP considers whether it is necessary or proper to make an application.

Two doctors make recommendations following personal examination of the patient either together or, if separately, within set time frames. Guidance recommends patients being seen jointly by the AMHP and at least one of the doctors, and that both doctors should discuss the case with the person considering making the application (Code para 14.45-46). The doctors must be independent of each other, and regulations set out potential conflicts of interest to be avoided (s.12A and conflict of interest regulations 2008).

Section 12 of the Act requires that one of these medical recommendations shall be given by a practitioner approved

> as having special experience in the diagnosis and treatment of mental disorder and unless that practitioner has previous acquaintance with the patient, the other such recommendation shall, if practicable, be given by a registered medical practitioner who has such previous acquaintance.

At least one but ideally both of the recommending medical practitioners must be so approved unless it is an emergency. Section 12 also states that at least one doctor should, if practicable, have previous acquaintance with the patient. This was considered in *AR v Bronglais Hospital* [2001] and requires that the doctor should 'have some previous knowledge of the patient and must not be coming to him or her cold, as it were'.

It would be necessary for an AMHP to explain on the application why it was not practicable to use a doctor who knew the patient. It may be appropriate on occasion to use doctors without previous acquaintance where the doctors have particular expertise in an area of practice, such as forensic services (*TTM v LB Hackney* [2011]).

The AMHP should ensure that where a patient is known to belong to a specific group, such as under 18s, a patient with a learning disability or autism, older adults or those with dementia, at least one of the professionals involved in the assessment has expertise in working with people from that group, wherever possible (Code para 14.39).

Medical recommendations form the basis for applications to hospital. Code guidance stipulates that the AMHP is usually the preferred applicant (rather than the NR) because of professional training, knowledge of law and resources, and because this avoids the risk of adversely affecting the relationship between the relative and patient if the nearest relative were to make an application (Code para 14.30).

The AMHP has a duty in s.11(3) to take such steps as are practicable to inform the person (if any) appearing to be the NR 'before or within a reasonable time after an application has been made' that either the application is to be or has been made and of the NR's powers to order the discharge of the relative.

Section 4 – admission for assessment in cases of emergency

Section 4 is essentially an application for admission for assessment (as per s.2) with one medical recommendation, on the basis that there is urgent necessity to make the application and that waiting for the second medical recommendation for the s.2 would cause an undesirable delay. Section 4 lasts for up to 72 hours, cannot be renewed and will end unless a second medical recommendation is supplied to convert it to s.2. Patients on s.4 are not subject to Part IV and cannot be treated under compulsion.

Instances where it may be used include

> immediate and significant risk of mental or physical harm to the patient or to others; danger of serious harm to property; or a need for the use of restrictive interventions on the patient.
>
> (Code para 15.8)

The process for applications remains the same as for s.2, as does the AMHP's duty to inform the NR where the AMHP is the applicant.

Section 3 – admission for treatment

Section 3 provides for patients to be admitted for treatment of a mental disorder for up to six months. Section 3 is renewable for a further six months and then annually (s.20). The RC must examine the patient within the final two months of detention, consult with another professional (from a different profession to that of the RC) who is concerned with the patient's medical treatment, and have that professional's agreement in writing that conditions are satisfied for renewal of the s.3. In practice, this could be a social worker or care coordinator but in any event has to be someone directly involved in the treatment of the patient.

Grounds. The legal grounds for admission under section 3:

> S.3(2) An application for admission for treatment may be made in respect of a patient on the grounds that
>
> (a) he is suffering from mental disorder of a nature or degree which makes it appropriate for him to receive medical treatment in a hospital; and
>
> (b) [...]
>
> (c) it is necessary for the health or safety of the patient or for the protection of other persons that he should receive such treatment and it cannot be provided unless he is detained under this section; and
>
> (d) appropriate medical treatment is available for him.

As discussed in Chapter 2, a learning disability where no other mental disorder is present is not to be treated as a mental disorder for the purposes of the s.3 grounds unless associated with abnormally aggressive or seriously irresponsible conduct on the patient's part (s.1(2A)) and s.1(2b)(a)).

Procedure. The process, timescales for recommendations, and requirements of previous acquaintance and s.12 approval are the same as for section 2. However, for s.3 the medical recommendations are required to specify that appropriate treatment is available. This requires the recommendations to state at which hospitals the appropriate treatment will be available. It is the doctor's role to locate the appropriate bed (Code para 14.77) unless local policy indicates otherwise. Appropriate treatment is considered in more detail in Chapter 6.

Applications. The process of making the application for s.3 is largely as per s.2 above. Two medical recommendations form the basis for an application to be made.

However, the AMHP is unable to make an application for s.3 (or for s.7 guardianship) if the NR objects to the application being made or if the AMHP has not consulted with the NR.

Nature and degree. As we have seen in Chapter 2, the ECtHR has held that unsoundness of mind must be of a 'kind or degree' to warrant compulsory confinement (*Winterwerp v Netherlands* [1979]). This is reflected in the phrase 'nature or degree' in the above sections of the MHA.

Detention could be based on either nature or degree, or both. Code guidance summarises the findings of the court in *R v MHRT* [1999]:

> Nature refers to the particular mental disorder from which the patient is suffering, its chronicity, its prognosis and the patient's previous responses to receiving treatment for the disorder. Degree refers to the current manifestations of the patient's disorder.
>
> (para 14.6)

Health or safety or protection of other persons

Medical recommendations for s.2 and s.3 require that the examining doctors indicate under which of these grounds the patient is to be detained. Note again that this can be for health or safety or protection of others. Although recommendations can say that two or all three of the grounds are met, one would suffice.

Chapter 14 of the Code offers additional guidance on what factors should be considered when deciding whether patients should be detained on health or safety grounds. These include consideration of harm to self, suicide, self-neglect or jeopardising their own health or safety accidentally, recklessly or unintentionally (Code para 14.9). In considering protection of others, the Code lists factors to consider, including the likelihood that harm will result and the severity of any potential harm, taking account of history and evidence as well as the reliability of both. The Code also recommends that professionals consider the willingness and ability of those living with the patient to cope and manage such a risk and any potential harm to them (Code para 14.10).

On-the-spot questions	When might a person be detained on s.2 or s.3 on the basis of the 'nature' of their illness and not degree? What should professionals take into account in making such a decision?

Risks of admission

Unfortunately, admission to a psychiatric hospital does not necessarily protect the patient from harm. Although statistics indicate a reduction in psychiatric in-patient suicides, these still happen. The *National Confidential Inquiry into Suicide and Homicide by People with Mental Illness* reports on an annual basis on in-patient deaths, including suicide, either as an in-patient or following absconding from the ward. Although in-patient suicide rates in England have fallen (2015), 1295 in-patient deaths by suicide occurred between 2003 and 2013.

The case of *Savage v South Essex Partnership* [2008] established that a hospital has an obligation to take steps to protect the life of a detained patient who presents a 'real and immediate risk' of suicide.

In *Rabone v Pennine Care* [2012], the Supreme Court ruled that the same duty may be owed to an informal patient, depending on the presence of relevant factors such as the assumption of responsibility for the individual's welfare by the State, the victim's vulnerability and the nature of the risk.

Chapter 14 of the Code also summarises issues which should be balanced in all cases when admission is being considered:

> The impact that any future deterioration or lack of improvement in the patient's condition would have on their children, other relatives or carers, especially those living with the patient, including an assessment of their ability and willingness to cope, and the effect on the patient and those close to the patient, of a decision to admit or not to admit under the Act.

> (para 14.8)

Section 2 or section 3

Figures from the Health and Social Care Information Centre annual report for England indicate that section 2 admissions have increased by 9.7 per cent in 2014–15 (HSCIC 2015). This mirrors increases in previous years from 2009–10 to 2013–14.

There was a reported gradual decline in use of s.3 from 2009–14 (HSCIC 2014). However, recent statistics from the HSCIC show an increase of 17.1 per cent in use of s.3 following an informal admission.

Both sections allow for the treatment of mental disorder, and Hale (2010) suggests that s.2 is 'in keeping with the least restrictive principle'. Jones (2015) also states that

> practitioners' choice of section should be guided by the least restriction principle … [and] a patient whose current mental health

and circumstances require him to be subject to the very significant procedure of compulsory detention surely needs to be assessed however well known he might be to the mental health service.

The increase in use of s.2 has caused some debate, including concern over increased workloads for AMHPs, recommending doctors and those involved in Mental Health Tribunals. It is interesting to note that following this debate, there have been some revisions in the 2015 English Code which appear to pull back slightly from the emphasis on s.2, as follows (revisions in italics):

> **KEY CASE ANALYSIS**

Chapter 14 Code guidance on use of section 2 and section 3. Section 2 should *only* be used if

- the full extent of the nature and degree of a patient's condition is unclear;
- there is a need to carry out an initial in-patient assessment in order to formulate a treatment plan, or to reach a judgement about whether the patient will accept treatment on a voluntary basis following admission; or
- There is a need to carry out a new in-patient assessment in order to reformulate a treatment plan, or to reach a judgement about whether the patient will accept treatment on a voluntary basis.

Section 3 should be used if

- The patient is already detained under section 2 (detention under section 2 cannot be renewed by a new section 2 application); or
- The nature and current degree of the patient's mental disorder, the essential elements of the treatment plan to be followed and the likelihood of the patient accepting treatment as an informal patient are already *sufficiently* established *to make it unnecessary to undertake a new assessment under section 2.*

The rationale for decisions to use section 2 or section 3 should be clearly recorded.

On-the-spot question

When might it be appropriate to consider an assessment for s.2 when a patient is already known to mental health services?

> **KEY CASE ANALYSIS**

Note that this case refers to the 'ASW' as it pre-dates the 2007 MHA amendments.

R (Von Brandenburg) v E London and City Mental Health NHS Trust [2003] UKHL 58

The question for the court in this case was this:

> When a Mental Health Review Tribunal has ordered the discharge of a patient, is it lawful to re-admit him under section 2 or section 3 of the Mental Health Act 1983 where it cannot be demonstrated that there has been a relevant change of circumstances?

Mr Brandenburg was detained on s.2 MHA. He appealed against his section to the Mental Health Review Tribunal. Although the doctor was resistant to discharge, the Tribunal ordered the discharge of Mr Brandenburg. This discharge was deferred for seven days in order to allow for community services to be set up, including accommodation and a care plan to include medication.

The day before the due discharge date, while still in hospital, medical recommendations for further detention under s.3 were made by the same doctors who had recommended the s.2. An application was then made by the same ASW who had applied for the s.2 and had attended the Tribunal.

The House of Lords (now Supreme Court) ruled that 'an ASW may not lawfully apply for the admission of a patient whose discharge has been ordered by the decision of a Mental Health Tribunal of which the ASW is aware unless the ASW has formed the reasonable and bona fide opinion that he has information not known to the Tribunal which puts a significantly different complexion on the case as compared with that which was before the Tribunal'.

The judge gives some examples of situations where it may be lawful to make an application for detention following discharge by the Tribunal; these include professionals being made aware of a risk to the patient or others as a result of suicide, self-harm or refusal to take medication or a deterioration in mental state which significantly changes the risk picture. The crucial issue is that the information must have been unknown to the Tribunal and significantly change the situation as it was presented to the Tribunal.

The judgment emphasises the importance of the ASW in protecting individual human rights:

> *I would … resist the lumping together of the ASW and the recommending doctor or doctors as 'the mental health professionals'. It is the ASW who makes the application, not the doctors.*

Informal patients and the Mental Capacity Act

In 2014–15, in England, nearly 1.8 million people were in contact with secondary mental health services each year and 103,840 (5.7%) of those became in-patients (HSCIC 2015).

Many people use secondary mental health services without requiring an admission or may agree to an admission to hospital without the need for detention under the MHA. This is generally seen as the least restrictive option simply because it does not amount to a deprivation of liberty.

Section 131 of the MHA provides the option of admission to hospital without the need for detention or for patients to remain in hospital 'informally' once detention has ended by whatever means. Although the terms 'informal admission' and 'voluntary admission' are sometimes used interchangeably, they do not amount to the same thing.

Voluntary admission implies that the patient volunteers and understands the necessary issues in an admission to a psychiatric ward. The notion of 'informality' is based upon the Mental Treatment Act 1930, which allowed for patients to bring themselves to hospital without the need for a formal 'certification' processes.

As Hale (2010) states:

> Theoretically, at least, informal patients enjoy two legal rights which detained patients do not. They may leave hospital whenever they like and they may refuse to accept any form of treatment which they do not want.

Professionals need to guard against admissions based upon coercion, which might result in no choice at all and be open to challenge on their legality. Patients must understand enough to make an informed choice whether to enter hospital and all that may entail (*A PCT v LDV* [2013]).

Informal admission could apply to those with or without capacity to consent to the necessary admission and assessment or treatment. For those patients who are assessed as lacking capacity for this decision at the time it needs to be made, the MCA would provide for their informal admission as long as it was in their best interests and professionals have followed ss.1–4 MCA. However, although such an admission can include the use of restraint (ss.5–6 MCA), it cannot amount to a deprivation of liberty. This is explored in more detail in Chapter 8.

On-the-spot question	What information do you think it would be necessary to give someone in order for the person to decide whether to consent to an admission to a psychiatric hospital?

Applications in respect of patients already in hospital

Commonly referred to as 'holding powers', this section provides emergency powers to doctors and approved clinicians and nurses of a prescribed class to hold the patient on the ward until a full assessment can be arranged with the necessary doctors and AMHP.

Section 5(4) grounds. This section applies to psychiatric in-patients only:

> S.5(4) If, in the case of a patient who is receiving treatment for mental disorder as an in-patient in a hospital, it appears to a nurse of the prescribed class.
>
> > (a) that the patient is suffering from mental disorder to such a degree that it is necessary for his health or safety or for the protection of others for him to be immediately restrained

PRACTICE FOCUS

Rebecca is 74 years old and has a history of anxiety and depression. She had a series of cognitive behaviour therapy (CBT) sessions a year ago via her GP, but there are now significant concerns for her safety. She has increasing symptoms of serious depression, with early-morning wakening, difficulty in sleeping and eating, suicidal thoughts and some increasing confusion.

Her GP believes that she may require an admission to psychiatric hospital. Rebecca has never been admitted to hospital before and is anxious about what this may entail.

What might be the least restrictive options that would maximise Rebecca's independence?

If Rebecca requires an admission, what are the available options?

Table 3.2: Holding Powers – Summary

Section	Duration	Consent to Treatment Provisions Applies (Part IV)?	Access to Mental Health Tribunal?	Nearest Relative Powers
S.5(2) – application in respect of a patient already in hospital	Up to 72 hours from time of report being furnished	No	No	None
S.5(4) – as above	Up to six hours from when recorded in writing	No	No	None

> from leaving the hospital; and (b) that it is not practicable to secure the immediate attendance of a practitioner for the purpose of furnishing a report under subsection (2) above.

This allows for a psychiatric in-patient to be detained for a period of no more than six hours from the time when the above is recorded. Nurses of a prescribed class might use this power where a patient has stated the intent to leave the ward; the other grounds above are met; and the medical practitioner or approved clinician in charge of treatment is not immediately available. The doctor should examine the patient within the six hours to determine whether to use s.5(2).

Section 5(2) grounds.

> S.5(2) If, in the case of a patient who is an in-patient in a hospital, it appears to the registered medical practitioner [or approved clinician] in charge of the treatment of the patient that an application ought to be made under this Part of this Act for the admission of the patient to hospital, he may furnish to the managers a report in writing to that effect: and in any such case the patient may be detained in the hospital for a period of 72 hours from the time when the report is so furnished.

An in-patient can be detained for up to 72 hours under this power. He or she need not be a psychiatric in-patient and could be a patient on a general ward requiring further assessment under the MHA. If a patient is medically fit for discharge from a general ward for example, but requires further assessment for mental disorder, this section may be used. Arrangements for further assessment should be put in place as soon as possible from the start of the s.5(2). The outcome of the assessment should be recorded, as should timescales. Patients are not subject to Part IV consent to treatment provisions and cannot be treated compulsorily. Treatment, therefore, can only be given with their consent, or in some cases, in their best interests (s.4 MCA).

Patients who are admitted informally or under the MCA may find themselves subject to s.5 at any time during their admission if the above grounds are met. It is easy to see why patients might be confused by their legal status once admitted, and those using the powers must ensure that they are not used in a coercive or punitive manner and that patients are given their rights under s.132. This raises the issue of what constitutes an informal admission and what are genuinely least restrictive options. The use of section 5 should be monitored by hospital managers (Code para 18.39).

Police powers

These sections provide the police with the power to remove someone to a 'place of safety'; in the case of s.135, from private premises and from a

Table 3.3: Police Powers – Summary

Section	Duration	Consent to Treatment Provisions Applies (Part IV)?	Access to Mental Health Tribunal?	Nearest Relative Powers
S.135(1) – warrant to search for and remove patients	Not exceeding 72 hours (including any transfer between places of safety)	No	No	None
S.135(2) – warrant to search for and remove patients	Not exceeding 72 hours (including any transfer between places of safety)	No	No	None
S.136 – mentally disordered persons found in a public place	Not exceeding 72 hours	No	No	None

public place in the case of s.136. Detention at the place of safety can last for up to 72 hours if certain grounds are met. A review of s.135 and s.136 in 2014 (DH 2014c) recommended changes to some aspects of these powers. The Policing and Crime Bill 2015–16 reflects this and proposes several changes to s.135 and s.136, discussed below.

Section 135(6) defines a place of safety as

> residential accommodation provided by a local authority under Part I of the Care Act 2014, a hospital, a police station, a care home or any other suitable place where the occupier is willing temporarily to receive the patient.

A police station should not be used as a place of safety unless the circumstances are exceptional (such as risky behaviour) (Code 16.38). Local policies should set out where these places may be.

Section 135 – warrant to search for and remove patients

The legal grounds for the issuing of a s.135(1) warrant are

> S.135(1) If it appears to a justice of the peace, on information on oath laid by an approved mental health professional, that there is reasonable cause to suspect that a person believed to be suffering from mental disorder
>
> > (a) has been, or is being, ill-treated, neglected or kept otherwise than under proper control, in any place within the jurisdiction of the justice, or
> >
> > (b) being unable to care for himself, is living alone in any such place,
>
> the justice may issue a warrant authorising any constable to enter, if need be by force, any premises specified in the warrant in which that person is believed to be, and, if thought fit, to remove him to a place of safety with a view to the making of an application in respect of him under Part II of this Act, or of other arrangements for his treatment or care.

Procedure. An AMHP has to provide information on oath for s.135(1). If the application is granted a constable may execute the warrant.

Section 135(1) is commonly misunderstood by AMHPs as requiring evidence of a refusal of permission to enter the premises before an application to the Justice of the Peace can be made. However, these are not the grounds for applying under s.135(1), although access may be part of the issue. It would therefore be acceptable to apply for a warrant without first trying to gain access as long as the documented reasons could explain why this was proportionate and justified. The information may include, for example, why the powers in s.115, to enter and inspect any premises in which a mentally disordered patient is living, are insufficient. There may be concerns, for example, that someone on the premises is likely to be violent or run away immediately on entry.

Section 135(1) and the accompanying warrant authorise a constable to enter the specified premises with an AMHP and a registered medical practitioner, 'if need be by force', and to remain there for the purposes set out above. This is a significant power and can be experienced as quite traumatising by patients (Watson and Daley 2015).

It may seem draconian to have a power in the MHA that allows police entrance to a person's private abode without that person's consent and to remove him or her even though the person has not committed a crime. It certainly engages the person's A8 right to respect for private and family life:

> [T]he house of every one is to him as his castle and fortress, as well as for his defence against injury and violence, as for his repose.
>
> *(Semayne's Case* [1604]*)*

However, Article 8 ECHR is not an absolute right. Article 8(2) states that

> there shall be no interference by a public authority with the exercise of this right except such as in accordance with the law and is necessary in a democratic society in the interests of national security, public safety or the economic wellbeing of the country, for the prevention of disorder or crime, for the protection of health or morals, or for the protection of the rights and freedom of others.

Therefore, information on oath for the application of a s.135(1) warrant must set out why such a power is necessary and a proportionate intervention in the individual case, what harm may come to the person or others and why other means of assessing their needs are inadequate. It is likely that a Justice of the Peace will question the AMHP accordingly, and the AMHP should be well prepared to answer such questions when providing the information on oath (see Code para 16.11).

Justices of the Peace are not obliged to issue such a warrant and less likely to do so if the information and evidence provided is insufficient.

Such applications to the court should be closed to the public. It is also reasonable to assume that a patient may access such information by making any request under the Freedom of Information Act (2000).

This warrant gives the AMHP, registered medical practitioner and constable authority to enter premises and, 'if thought fit', remove the patient to a place of safety for assessment to take place in order to provide medical recommendations and an application to be made under s.2 or s.3, or for making other arrangements for the patient's treatment or care to be made, for example arranging an assessment under the Care Act 2014.

There is no explicit right in s.135(1) to remain on the premises to undertake this assessment. In some circumstances, the AMHP and doctor in attendance might proceed to a fuller assessment while at the premises. The DH review recommended amending s.135 to make it clear that the AMHP and doctor could remain on the premises to undertake a full MHA assessment. The revised Code of Practice added the following guidance:

> The AMHP and the doctor may convene a mental health assessment in the person's home if it is safe and appropriate to do so and the person consents to this. In taking this decision, consideration should be given as to who else is present, particularly if a person might be distressed by the assessment taking place in these circumstances.
>
> (para 16.8)

This section allows for the transfer of the person from one place of safety to another within the 72 hours. This may be used, for example, where someone is in a place of safety far from home and local services know the person and would provide a fuller assessment, or where a young person should be in a specialist unit for the assessment.

In practice, many people may open their door when they hear that police are at their premises with the AMHP and doctor. They may not understand why such a power applies to them or may be fearful of the implications of police presence. The troubling issue of neighbours being in earshot or within sight of this process does nothing to lessen the potential stigma associated with the use of this power. Others may be so frightened by symptoms of psychosis, for example, that they are unable to respond, and the use of force is necessary to gain entry to establish what should happen next.

Professionals should tread lightly and ensure they treat the person with respect and dignity and do all they can to ensure respect for their privacy. The warrant must be served on the person if it is executed. If it transpires that the person is not inside, the warrant must be left for the person to see. The Care Act retains a duty on the local authority to 'take reasonable steps to prevent or mitigate the loss or damage to moveable property' (s.47(2)) and s.58, The Social Services & Wellbeing (Wales) Act 2014).

S.135(2) refers to taking or retaking a patient who is liable under this Act and when there is reasonable cause to believe that the person is to be found on the premises and that admission has been or is likely to be refused. This refers to patients who have absconded from detention or are absent without leave (AWOL) or who have taken themselves away from somewhere they are required to reside (e.g. under a s.7 guardianship order). It need not be an AMHP who applies for a s.135(2) warrant, and the constable need not be accompanied by an AMHP or doctor in the execution of it.

Care coordinators may be required to make applications to court for s.135(2) warrants and to accompany the constable in the execution of the warrant. Local policies should be available to guide care coordinators for s.135(2) applications and AMHPs for s.135(1).

Section 136 – mentally disordered persons found in public places

This gives the police power to take someone to a place of safety on the following grounds:

> S.136(1) If a constable finds in a place to which the public have access a person who appears to him to be suffering from mental disorder and to be in immediate need of care or control, the constable may, if he thinks it necessary to do so in the interests of that person or for the protection of other persons, remove that person to a place of safety within the meaning of section 135.

A public place means 'a place to which the public have open access, access if a payment is made or access at certain times of the day' (Code para 16.18). This could be a pub, park, library or sports centre and may include parts of Accident and Emergency where the public have access. Staff working in hospitals should be aware of which parts are public and which are not.

Procedure. The purpose of this section is for police to take someone to a place of safety for up to 72 hours in order that the person can be examined by a doctor and interviewed by an AMHP, with a view to 'making suitable arrangements for his treatment or care'. The person need not have committed an offence.

Once at the place of safety, if the doctor concludes there is no mental disorder, then immediate discharge should follow. Article 5 ECHR relies on the presence of mental disorder for further detention to be lawful. For this reason, the Royal College of Psychiatrists (RCP) made recommendations in 2013 that the AMHP and doctor should attend the place of safety 'within 3 hours in all cases where there are not good clinical grounds to delay assessment' (RCP 2013), thus ensuring that the person is not detained for longer than absolutely necessary using these emergency powers. This is now reflected in the Code, which sets out at para 16.47 that 'it is good practice for the doctor and the AMHP to attend within 3 hours'. Clearly, there may be occasions where the patient requires a longer period of time before being interviewed in a suitable manner or examination of the patient is appropriate (such as intoxication), but such reasons should be recorded.

If the person is deemed to have a mental disorder, the AMHP and doctor may then conclude that informal admission is appropriate, or admission under s.2 or s.3 is required. Where admission is not required, the AMHP should still make social care inquiries and any necessary arrangements for the person (e.g. referral for an assessment under the Care Act 2014 for the person and any carer).

S.136 also allows the use of reasonable force if necessary and proportionate in the care, control and conveying of the patient (s.137(2)).

The police are not psychiatrists and are not expected to show the same level of skill in determining whether someone has a mental disorder. Section 136 only requires that it appear to the constable that the person is suffering from mental disorder and is in immediate need of care or control.

A public place does not include private premises, such as the person's own residence or private homes belonging to others. It is not appropriate to encourage a person outside in order to use section 136 powers (Code para 16.18). A public place does not include a person's front garden or car, although the DH (2014c) proposed that s.136 be amended and apply anywhere except a private home. This is also proposed in the Policing and Crime Bill 2015–16.

Section 136 is an arrest under the Police and Criminal Evidence Act 1984. Code C of this Act requires rights to be given to the person, including, if at a police station, access to a solicitor.

In their 2012–13 MHA monitoring report, the Care Quality Commission raised concern that such an arrest could be divulged as part of a Criminal Records Bureau disclosure. The CQC referred to MP Charles Walker raising this issue in the House of Commons in 2011–12. The Home Office response is cited in the CQC report: 'on its own, information relating to physical health or mental health is unlikely to be appropriate for disclosure' (CQC 2014).

Police stations as places of safety. Use of s.136 in England increased from 14,111 in 2010–11 to 19,403 in 2014–15 (HSCIC).

Police stations were still being used as places of safety for s.136 in England in 6028 cases in 2013–14 (HSCIC). Although this is a downward trend from 8667 in 2011–12, it remains of concern given the Code guidance at para 16.38 that police stations should not be used as a place of safety except in exceptional circumstances. Furthermore, police cells can be experienced as criminalising mental disorder and potentially exacerbating the stigma that people experience.

Police services have raised concerns about the use of police stations as places of safety (DH 2014c). The CQC (2014) also raised concern at the over-use of police cells as places of safety because of inadequacies in accessing health-based places of safety:

> [W]hile some health-based places of safety are effective, others are less responsive to people's needs and require far reaching improvements.

They report that this is the case because health-based places of safety are full and therefore

> turn people away because they cannot meet demand, or they may be turning people away due to policies of not taking children or young people, not taking anyone with disturbed behaviour or if they are intoxicated.

Police are then left with the difficulties of taking the person to the police station when no other option is left. The CQC goes on to state:

> While we have heard from many individuals who have told us that the police were very kind and compassionate, police stations can be stressful places, and healthcare can be more difficult to access than in a health-based location. In 2011/12 and 2012/13, people with mental health problems accounted for half of all deaths in or following police custody (seven out of 15 deaths in both years),

and over a third in 2013/14 (four out of 11). Of these 18 deaths, five people had been detained under the MHA.

There was particular concern in the report about the availability of health-based places of safety for those under 18 years. Under s.136, 753 children and young people under age 18 were detained in 2013–14. Of these 236 were detained in police cells (31%).

The limited availability of health-based places of safety for under 18s and access to CAMHS services has contributed to this problem (DH 2014c).

However, annual statistics from 2014–15 do show a reduction in the use of police cells as a place of safety (HSCIC) following the concerns raised above.

The recently announced Policing and Crime Bill 2015–16 proposes changes to the MHA including:

- that children and young people under 18 are never taken to police cells if detained under ss.135 or 136, ensuring that police cells only be used as a place of safety if behaviour was so extreme it could not otherwise be managed.
- reducing the length of detention from 72 to 24 hours.

Black and minority ethnic (BME) groups remain over-represented in detention rates, and s.136 is no exception (HSCIC 2015).

The Code emphasises the need for locally agreed policies which should include effective monitoring on circumstances and outcomes of use of s.136, including in relation to BME communities and others with a protected characteristic as defined in the Equality Act 2010 (para 16.33). The 2012 Welsh Good Practice Guidance on s.135 and s.136 states that local policies

> should clearly define each agency's responsibility, environmental expectations and risk-management standards, how the operation of the policy will be monitored and the timeframe for its review.
> (para 11)

The Department of Health funded a pilot of 'street triage' schemes in England whereby mental health professionals provide police officers with 'on the spot' advice to deal with incidents involving people with mental health problems. In areas where this has been operating, there has been a reduction in the use of s.136 (DH 2014a).

It may be that the person subject to s.136 has also been arrested for an offence. In this case, it may be necessary for police to arrange an

> **KEY CASE ANALYSIS** <

MS v United Kingdom 24527/08 [2012] ECHR 804

In this case, a severely mentally ill man was detained under s.136 and held in a police cell for a period of more than 72 hours. His behaviour deteriorated rapidly throughout his stay. He was described as 'shouting, banging the door, lowering his trousers, licking the wall of his cell, hitting his head against the wall, smearing himself with food or faeces and drinking from the toilet bowl'. The issue at stake was that although two doctors had recommended admission following examination on 6 December, the police and the AMHP were unable to secure the appropriate psychiatric hospital bed and therefore arrange the necessary admission. A hospital bed was eventually found. The man was assessed as having a diagnosis of manic episode with psychotic features, given rapid tranquilisation and seclusion and continued medication. He showed 'sustained improvement' over the following days. The police were not criticised for their treatment of MS, even though the conditions 'were an affront to human dignity and reached the thresholds of degrading treatment for the purposes of Article 3'.

appropriate adult under the Police and Criminal Evidence Act Codes of Practice. In practice, this can often be the care coordinator and could be the social worker of the client in custody. The role of appropriate adult is discussed in more detail in Chapter 5.

> **On-the-spot question**   Why do you think s.136 has been increasing?

Further reading

Care Quality Commission (CQC) (2015) *Monitoring the Mental Health Act in 2013/14.* Annual report on the use of the MHA in England.

The Commission to Review the Provision of Acute Inpatient Psychiatric Care for Adults (2015) *Improving Acute Inpatient Psychiatric Care for Adults in England – Interim Report.* This is a very topical review, suggesting that the current reported bed crisis is linked to a problem with discharges from hospital, among other issues. The final report is due for publication in early 2016. More information can be found at www.caapc.info.

Department of Health (DH), Home Office (2014c) *Review of the Operation of Sections 135 and 136 of the Mental Health Act 1983 – Review Report and Recommendations*.

Health Inspectorate Wales (2015) *Monitoring the Use of the Mental Health Act in 2013–2014*. Annual report on the use of the MHA in Wales.

Health and Social Care Information Centre (2015c) *Mental Health Bulletin: Annual Statistics 2014 to 2015*. Detail on patient groups, age, gender, ethnicity and use of the MHA.

4

COMPULSION IN THE COMMUNITY

AT A GLANCE THIS CHAPTER COVERS:

- leave of absence (s.17)
- community treatment orders (CTOs) (s.17A)
- guardianship (s.7)
- aftercare (s.117)

Table 4.1: Compulsion in the Community – Summary

Section	Duration	Consent to Treatment Provisions Apply (Part IV)?	Access to Mental Health Tribunal?	Nearest Relative Powers
S.17 – leave of absence from hospital	Cannot go beyond the period of detention but duration is at the discretion of the RC	Yes	Yes, as per underlying section	As per underlying section
S.17A – community treatment order	Up to six months, can be extended by six months then annually	Part 4A applies	Yes, within first six months and then in every period of CTO. Automatic hearing after first six months if no application made or if CTO is revoked	Power to order the discharge of the relative (s.23), but note RC can block using s.25
S.7 – reception into guardianship	Up to six months, renewable for six months and then annually	No	Yes, in first six months and then every period of guardianship; automatic hearing if no application made in second six months	NR can object to a guardianship order. NR also has the power to order discharge, and there is no barring order available to stop this

The MHA provides for compulsion in the community for certain patients, and there is also a duty upon the local authority, clinical commissioning group or health board to provide aftercare for patients who are liable to be detained or are discharged from detention under certain sections.

Leave of absence (s.17)

Patients who are detained in hospital for assessment and/or treatment (some Part II or non-restricted Part III patients) can only leave hospital with permission of their RC. For restricted patients, leave has to be approved by the Secretary of State for Justice.

Granting leave of absence from the hospital is usually part of a longer-term plan towards discharge. As such, it should be part of planning and involve the patient, even though the patient need not consent to it. It cannot be underestimated how important many patients view the opportunity to have leave from hospital.

S.17(1) states that the RC may grant to any patient who is for the time being liable to be detained in a hospital under this part of this Act, leave to be absent from the hospital subject to such conditions (if any) as that clinician considers necessary in the interest of the patient or for the protection of other persons.

The RC can grant leave under s.17 for limited periods or for extended periods of time as long as it does not go past the period of detention.

Conditions of leave

The RC can specify conditions while the patient is on leave. These could include going out for a specified length of time with an escort, or alone, to the local shops or back home overnight; duration of leave; what treatment the patient is required to adhere to; and contact with professionals during their leave. It can involve longer-term leave of absence with weekly returns to the ward to report on progress, for example if the patient is on a trial period at a residential home, or indeed to another hospital. S.17(3) states

> where it appears to the RC that it is necessary to do so in the interests of the patient or for the protection of other persons he may, upon granting leave of absence . . .direct that the patient remain in custody during his absence.

The RC remains responsible for the patient on leave in the same way as if the patient were on the ward.

The patient can be in the custody of anyone authorised by the managers of the hospital, which is often, in reality, nursing staff. Leave conditions should be in writing and made clear to the patient. Nursing staff have discretion about whether to grant the leave on any given day, and this is made clear by the RC, who may, for example, review leave on a weekly basis.

Code guidance states that leave of absence can be 'an important part of a detained patients care plan but can also be a time of risk' (para 27.10). For this reason, the RC is advised to consider the benefits and any risks to the patient's health and safety, how leave may facilitate the patient's recovery, conditions that should be attached, child protection and welfare issues, support required while on leave, contingency plans and community services available.

The Code indicates that long-term leave should be planned properly, patients should be involved in the decision, as should carers, family and community services (para 27.18). The CQC (2010) reported difficulties for some patients in accessing their leave as a result of nursing staffing levels. Good practice would indicate that care coordinators should be part of leave arrangements. In reality, the authors are aware of instances where relatives (and care coordinators) are unaware of leave being granted until a patient either alerts them or a family member is made aware by the patient returning home.

Crisis and Home Treatment Teams are often used as an aid to early discharge from detention and in assisting patients' reintegration back to their communities, with the aim of promoting recovery and maximising independence. However, research in *The National Confidential Inquiry into Suicide and Homicide by People with Mental Illness 2014* indicates that for some patients a longer period of in-patient stay, with the accompanying s.17 leave, may have been the more appropriate route:

> [S]uicide rates remain high compared with the in-patient set-
> ting, and safety of individuals cared for by crisis resolution home
> treatment teams should be a priority for mental health services.
> For some vulnerable people who live alone or have adverse life
> circumstances, CRHT might not be the most appropriate care set-
> ting. Use of CRHT teams to facilitate early discharge could present
> a risk to some patients, which should be investigated further.
>
> (*The Lancet* 2014)

Longer leave and consideration of CTO

Prior to the amendments to the MHA in 2007, s.17 leave was used for long periods of time (commonly termed 'long leave') in order to ascertain whether a patient was ready for discharge and to ensure that such discharge was likely to succeed, as in the case below.

> ⟩ **KEY CASE ANALYSIS** ⟨
>
> *R (CS) v Mental Health Review Tribunal* [2004] EWHC 2958 Admin
>
> The court considered the decision of the Tribunal to uphold the patient's detention while on 'long leave' from hospital. The patient had a history of psychotic illness and 'revolving door' admissions, characterised by lack of compliance with medication or services when she left hospital. At the time of the Tribunal, the patient was on 'long leave' at home, seeing her RC every four weeks at the hospital ward and a psychologist every week, along with her community team. The Tribunal did not discharge as it was believed that the patient still met the grounds for s.3 despite the long leave periods. The Tribunal accepted that a significant part of the patient's treatment plan and the RC's work towards discharge included this long leave. The RC had explained that in this patient's case it was not appropriate to abruptly discharge someone who had been detained on s.3 for some months; that such a discharge plan would be more likely to lead to deterioration and early readmission to hospital and in this patient's case a more serious deterioration and longer admission than if treated on long leave prior to discharge. The Tribunal decision was upheld by the court:
>
> > It is clear to me that the RMO was engaged in a delicate balancing exercise by which she was, with as light a touch as she could, encouraging progress to discharge. Her purpose was to break the persistent historical cycle of admission, serious relapse and readmission. It may be that in the closing stages of the treatment in hospital her grasp on the claimant was gossamer thin, but to view that grasp as insignificant is, in my view, to misunderstand the evidence.

Although it is still possible for a patient to be granted indefinite leave by the RC, s.17 now requires the RC to consider whether a community treatment order under s.17A would be more appropriate in cases where the RC is granting leave for more than seven consecutive days. As we shall see below, this may be one reason why the number of CTOs has far outweighed the Government's predictions.

Revoking leave and recalling patients

Once on leave, the patient remains 'liable to be detained'. The patient remains subject to Part IV consent to treatment rules and can be brought back to hospital at any time on the direction of the RC, for example where treatment is necessary or there are problems with leave.

The RC can recall the patient, if of the view that this is 'necessary for their health or safety or protection of others' to be recalled from leave. They must give notice in writing to the patient or whomever the patient is in the custody of, revoking the leave and recalling the patient to hospital. The decision is the RC's alone. The RC need not see the patient in order to recall the patient from leave and may be reliant on the up-to-date knowledge of care coordinators and family members who may see patients more regularly while they are at home on leave.

Leave and the informal patient

Patients who are not detained should be able to leave hospital at any time. 'They cannot be required to ask permission to do so, but may be asked to inform staff when they wish to leave the ward' (Code 27.38).

Community treatment orders (CTOs) (s.17A)

The statutory language of the community treatment order (CTO) provisions replicates that of s.17 leave, with the use of recall, revocation and conditions. However, the grounds and powers are different.

Patients who are eligible to be placed on a CTO are those already liable to be detained on sections 3, 37, 45A, 47 and 48. A CTO is an order for the patient's discharge from detention subject to the possibility of being recalled to hospital for further medical treatment. The original section under which the patient was liable to be detained is suspended and could be brought back into play if the CTO is revoked. For example, a patient who was detained under s.3 and is now on a CTO would return to detention under s.3 if the CTO was revoked. CTOs last for up to six months and can be extended for a further six months and then annually.

The RC may not make a CTO unless in his opinion the relevant criteria are met and an AMHP agrees in writing with that opinion and that it is appropriate to make the order.

Grounds

The relevant criteria for CTO are as follows:

> s.17A(5)
>
> (a) the patient is suffering from a mental disorder of a nature or degree which makes it appropriate for him to receive medical treatment;
> (b) it is necessary for his health or safety or for the protection of other persons that he should receive such treatment;
> (c) subject to his being liable to be recalled . . . such treatment can be provided without his continuing to be detained in hospital;
> (d) it is necessary that the RC should be able to exercise the power . . . to recall the patient to hospital; and
> (e) appropriate medical treatment is available for him.

Conditions attached to a CTO

Section 17B sets out the conditions to a CTO. There are two potential sets of conditions: mandatory and discretionary. The mandatory conditions, which are always part of a CTO, include that the patient must make himself available for examination by the RC for the purpose of evaluating whether the CTO should be extended and that the patient must make him- or herself available for examination if necessary by a second opinion appointed doctor (SOAD) for the purpose of certification under Part 4A (treatment).

Discretionary conditions may be specified by the RC but require agreement by an AMHP as necessary and appropriate to

- ensure that the patient receives medical treatment; or
- prevent risk of harm to the patients health or safety; or
- protect other persons.

Conditions may cover matters such as where and when the patient is to receive treatment in the community, where the patient is to live and avoidance of known risk factors or high-risk situations relevant to the patient's mental disorder, but they should be kept to a minimum in order to restrict the patient as little as possible. The rationale should be expressed clearly and linked to the care plan (Code ch. 29). Although there is no requirement for a patient to have capacity to consent to the CTO, it is most likely to work where patients are involved in formulating the conditions and can understand what is expected of them as well as what aftercare services will be provided.

Treatment on a CTO

Patients in the community who have not been recalled are subject to the consent to treatment rules in Part 4A (see Chapter 6). However, it is important to note that there is no power to compel treatment on a non-consenting, capacitous patient prior to recall.

Recall from CTO

The RC has the power to recall the patient under s.17E and need not have the agreement of the AMHP for this purpose. RCs may use recall if they are of the opinion that

(1)(a) The patient requires medical treatment in a hospital for his mental disorder and
(b) There would be a risk of harm to the health or safety of the patient or to others if the patient were not recalled to hospital for that purpose.

The RC may also recall the patient if he or she fails to comply with the mandatory conditions referred to above. Code guidance states:

> The recall power is intended to provide a means to respond to evidence of relapse or high-risk behaviour relating to mental disorder before the situation becomes critical and leads to the patient or other people being harmed. The need for recall might arise as a result of relapse, or by a change in the patient's circumstances giving rise to increased risk. The responsible clinician does not have to interview or examine the patient in person before deciding to recall them.
>
> (para 29.45)

Such action should be proportionate to the risk. It may, for example, be sufficient to monitor a patient in the community, in liaison with the care coordinator, or to encourage the patient, if consenting, to come to the hospital informally, without the need to recall. The care coordinator or family member may be the person who alerts the RC to possible deterioration in mental state. The patient himself may also alert services and be willing to attend the hospital site to talk with the RC, without the need for recall.

Where recall is necessary, it can be for a maximum of 72 hours to a hospital. Recall begins on arrival at the hospital, and patients are subject to Part IV consent to treatment provisions and can be treated compulsorily if necessary. Should the patient not respond to the recall notice once served, he is deemed to be absent without leave and can therefore be retaken to the hospital under s.18. Should it prove necessary to enter premises by force, a s.135(2) would be required.

During this 72-hour recall period, patients may be discharged back out to community services on the CTO or may agree to remain in hospital for a longer period informally, for example, in order to start a new medication or treatment plan; or they may have their CTO revoked. The recall period of 72 hours cannot be extended by a further recall notification. Within that time frame, the RC will have to consider whether to revoke the CTO, which requires the agreement of an AMHP.

Revoking the CTO

Revocation of the CTO under s.17F(4), as for s.17 leave, means that the patient is now detained once again on the underlying section. An AMHP must agree in writing that it is appropriate to revoke the order and that he is in agreement with the RC's opinion.

Grounds for revocation are exactly as they are for detention under s.3(2), that is, that the patient is

- suffering from mental disorder of a nature or degree which makes it appropriate for him to receive medical treatment in a hospital; and
- it is necessary for the health or safety of the patient or for the protection of other persons that he should receive such treatment, and it cannot be provided unless he is detained under this section; and
- appropriate medical treatment is available for him.

One of the main differences between s.17 leave and CTO recall and revocation is the RC alone makes decisions about s.17 leave. For CTOs, an AMHP is required for decisions about making the initial CTO, discretionary conditions, revocation and extension of the section. The patient no longer remains liable to be detained but is liable to be recalled, and it is the power of recall that has to be considered necessary for a CTO to be appropriately used.

> **PRACTICE FOCUS**
>
> Kasia has been subject to a CTO for the past three months. She has been told that if she stops her medication, she will be recalled to hospital.
>
> - What are the specific grounds for recall?
> - If Kasia is recalled and the RC wishes to revoke the CTO, what are the considerations for the AMHP?

The Code offers some pointers to the use of CTOs or s.17 leave in chapter 31:

Factors Suggesting Longer-term Leave	Factors Suggesting a CTO
<ul><li>Discharge from hospital is for a specific purpose or a fixed period.</li><li>The patient's discharge from hospital is deliberately on a 'trial' basis.</li><li>The patient is likely to need further in-patient treatment without their consent or compliance.</li><li>There is a serious risk of arrangements in the community breaking down or being unsatisfactory – more so than for a CTO.</li></ul>	<ul><li>There is confidence that the patient is ready for discharge from hospital on an indefinite basis.</li><li>There are good reasons to expect the patient will not need to be detained for the treatment they need to be given.</li><li>The patient appears prepared to consent or comply with the treatment they [sic] need – but risks as below mean that recall may be necessary.</li><li>The risk of arrangements in the community breaking down, or of the patient needing to be recalled to hospital for treatment, is sufficiently serious to justify a CTO, but not to the extent that it is very likely to happen.</li></ul>

> ***On-the-spot questions***
>
> When might it be more appropriate to use s.17A rather than s.17 long leave?
> What are the additional safeguards in the process of making a CTO?

Policy development and current issues with CTOs

The development of CTOs emphasised the needs of the 'revolving door' patient, described by the DH as those who

- are compulsorily admitted to hospital for treatment of mental illness;
- respond to treatment and improve;
- are discharged into the community with a care plan;
- fail to continue to comply with care plan and consequently deteriorate; and
- are formally readmitted to hospital, where the whole cycle begins again. (DH 1993)

As part of the consultation on the MH Bill, the Government commissioned a literature review, concluding that although some views were positive, there was

> currently no robust evidence about either the positive or negative effects of CTOs on key outcomes, including hospital readmission, length of hospital stay, improved medication compliance or patients' quality of life.
>
> (Churchill et al. 2007)

However, the Government introduced them in the amendments. Although the MHA uses the term 'CTO', the first Code of Practice to the amended Act referred to them as 'supervised community treatment', which caused some confusion. It did perhaps show the dilemma between patients' rights and public safety, with the use of 'order' traditionally referring to court directions rather than civil powers.

The Oxford Community Treatment Evaluation Trials (OCTET), from 2008–13 concluded that CTO use with patients with a psychotic disorder did not appear to reduce the rate of readmission or the overall hospital admission duration, nor did clinical or social functioning improve:

> We found no support in terms of any reduction in overall hospital admission to justify the significant curtailment of patients' personal liberty.
>
> (Burns et al. 2013)

In the same year, the MHA Post-legislative Scrutiny Report referred to this research and reported:

> The Committee does not object to the principle of CTO in defined circumstances . . . the Committee is, however, struck that the evidence base for this policy remains sparse, with the result that the argument had not developed far since the passage of the

legislation. The Committee recommends that the Department of Health should commission a fuller analysis of the value of a CTO in different clinician situations.

(DH 2007)

Various UK research studies show variable outcomes in clinical improvement, variable views from patients and professionals and concern over the balance between liberty and control and the use of CTOs:

> In light of all these difficulties with the research and the conflicting phenomena revealed in field studies of CTO regimes, it seems unlikely that the debate about them will be resolved by empirical means. In the end, people's views seem more likely to be influenced by judgements about the appropriate values or goals to be pursued by mental health law.

(Gostin 2010)

CTOs, therefore, have been a controversial addition to the MHA. The DH (2013) estimated there would be 450 CTOs in the first year, but within the first 17 months, 6241 CTOs had been made. Figures for use in England saw a year-on-year increase in the use of CTOs in the first five-year period, with a total of 4564 CTOs being made in the year 2014–15. These figures also show an even higher over-representation in their use with the black and black British communities than detention rates with this group (HSCIC 2015). As the AMHP's agreement is required before the RC can make a CTO, it is increasingly important for AMHPs to scrutinise their proposed use and consider both cultural and social perspectives when considering whether they are both appropriate and proportionate. Code principles of least restriction and maximising independence are highly relevant to CTOs.

On-the-spot questions	When might it be more appropriate to use a CTO rather than a long period of s.17 leave? What are the additional procedural requirements in the making of a CTO compared to the use of s.17 leave?

Guardianship (s.7)

Guardianship has a lower age limit of 16 years. It is not predominantly about treatment. It provides for a patient to be subject to guardianship either for the welfare of the patient or for the protection of others.

Guardianship applications are made to the local authority rather than the detaining hospital. Usually it is the local authority who will be the guardian, although s.7 also provides for private guardians to take on the role. Being received into guardianship does not require the patient to have first been detained. Where the local authority will be named as the guardian this will be delegated to a named worker, often a social worker in the team.

Grounds

> S.7(2) A guardianship application may be made in respect of a patient on the grounds that
>
> (a) he is suffering from mental disorder of a nature or degree which warrants his reception into guardianship under this section; and
>
> (b) it is necessary in the interests of the welfare of the patient or for the protection of other persons that the patient should be so received.

Note that as for s.3, for those who only have learning disability and no other mental disorder, the additional requirements of abnormally aggressive or seriously irresponsible conduct would have to apply for the grounds to be met for a guardianship order. This effectively rules out many adults with learning disabilities from the protection that guardianship may have offered, and although the MCA may have provided some solution, use of guardianship is not limited to incapacitated adults.

Procedure

An application for guardianship (s.7) requires two medical recommendations confirming the grounds above and an application to the local authority for the patient to be received into guardianship.

Powers

The guardian has three specific powers, to the exclusion of any other person:

> S.8(1)
>
> (a) the power to require the patient to reside at a place specified by the authority or person named as guardian;
>
> (b) the power to require the patient to attend at places and times so specified for the purpose of medical treatment, occupation, education or training;

(c) the power to require access to the patient to be given, at any place where the patient is residing, to any registered medical practitioner, [approved mental health professional] or other person so specified.

Part IV does not apply to guardianship patients as the emphasis is on welfare rather than overseeing medical treatment. It works well for patients who accept the authority of the guardian and can respond positively as a result of the structure placed upon them.

Guardianship has commonly been criticised for 'having no teeth' in relation to its efficacy to impose authority (e.g. Hale 2010). In part, this is because the requirement does not include a power to compel the patient to attend places specified, or access to those listed above. However, it can require them to reside at a specified place and take them back there should they absent themselves (s.18(7)). It does not authorise a deprivation of liberty, and in circumstances where the patient lacks capacity and is being deprived of their liberty, it would be necessary to apply for authorisation under the DoLS or from the Court of Protection (see Chapter 8).

Guardianship powers could, for example, be used to 'discourage the patient from living somewhere the Guardian considers unsuitable, breaking off contact with services, leaving the area before proper arrangements can be made and sleeping rough' (para 30.30).

The Code states:

> Guardianship therefore provides an authoritative framework for working with a patient, with a minimum of constraint, to achieve as independent a life as possible within the community. Where it is used, it should be part of the patient's overall care plan.
>
> (para 30.4)

It is a pity that its use has declined steadily over recent years. There was a decline of 37 per cent in use between 2004–5 and 2013–14. By 2014–15, it was in its tenth consecutive year of decline, albeit with annual figures increasing slightly in some years (HSCIC 2015). This overall decline may be due to the introduction of CTOs, or the DoLS. Chapter 30 of the Code suggests that where the patient lacks capacity to decide where to live, the Mental Capacity Act could be sufficient, and if need be, the DoLS or an application to the Court of Protection, without the need for guardianship at all.

However, guardianship is not exclusively for those who lack capacity, and may be used positively to ensure the welfare of capacitated patients or the protection of others. Case law has confirmed that guardianship may remain necessary even where a DoLS authorisation is in place, in instances where the power to return someone or protect the public is necessary, but not explicitly available through the DoLS regime (*Y County Council & ZZ* [2012]; *NM v Kent CC* [2015]).

The powers available to the NR are slightly enhanced in relation to guardianship; the AMHP has a duty to consult the NR for a guardianship order, and the NR has a right to object or indeed to order discharge (s.23), which cannot be blocked under s.25.

On-the-spot question	When might a guardianship order be more appropriate than a CTO?

Absence without leave (s.18)

Detained patients, those on recall from CTOs and some guardianship patients who are required to reside at a specified place but who then absent themselves from the hospital or place of residence without s.17 leave, are defined as absent without leave (AWOL) and can be brought back to the hospital in certain timescales, using s.18. Use of s.135(2) may be necessary if access to the premises is unlikely to be given.

Aftercare (s.117)

This section places a duty on the local authority and the clinical commissioning group (CCG) (in Wales, a local health board) to arrange to provide aftercare for certain patients (those on ss.3, 37, 45A, 47 and 48) once they cease to be detained. It also applies to those on s.17 leave while under those sections and those on CTOs.

The purpose of aftercare is to prevent readmission to hospital by providing support to patients and reducing the risk of deterioration in the patients' condition. S.75 of the Care Act 2014 introduced a definition of aftercare into s.117 as follows:

S.117(6)

- meeting a need arising from or related to the person's mental disorder; and

- reducing the risk of a deterioration of the person's mental condition (and, accordingly, reducing the risk of the person requiring admission to a hospital again for treatment for mental disorder).

Aftercare could apply to health care, social care, employment services and services to meet social or cultural needs or supported accommodation. However, this definition above requires a clear link between a need arising and the patient's mental disorder that requires aftercare services to reduce the risk of deterioration.

The Care Act also makes changes to the issue of ordinary residence and which local authority would be responsible for aftercare provision. In some cases, those placed in a care home, shared lives schemes or supporting living within England may remain the responsibility of the local authority where they resided prior to any placement there (s.39(1) Care Act 2014).

The Nationality Immigration and Asylum Act 2002 limits the support that local authorities can provide to asylum seekers and refugees. However, these exclusions do not apply to the provision of s.117 aftercare.

Housing has been one of the more significant issues in relation to the provision of s.117 aftercare. In *R (Mwanza) v LB Greenwich* [2010], the court held that housing provision that was not related to the persons mental disorder would not be covered by s.117. In the case of *R (Afework) v London Borough of Camden* [2013], the court went further in finding that 'basic' accommodation (such as a roof over one's head) could never be considered as part of s.117 aftercare, but that 'enhanced' accommodation such as specialist accommodation might be as long as it was to meet a need arising from the mental disorder. The Care Act amendments as above in s.117(6) would seem to point towards basic accommodation being unlikely to be covered within the meaning of aftercare. Guidance in chapter 33 of the Code recommends that local authorities and CCGs should interpret the meaning of aftercare broadly. It seems likely that further cases will be brought before the courts.

CCGs and Health Boards are also responsible for s.117 aftercare in relation to the provision of health care, and local social services authorities are responsible for the provision of social care. However, although s.117(2E) allows regulations to be used to ensure, for example, that the CCG responsible for s.117 aftercare is also the CCG commissioning other health services for the person, it may still be the case that a patient receives care from two different CCGs and an LSSA in yet another area.

S.117 remains complex and open to argument between agencies. Perhaps this is why the Care Act has inserted a provision for managing disputes in England at s.40 and in Wales at s.195 of the Social Services & Wellbeing (Wales) Act (Welsh Government & Department of Health 2015).

Risk and the Mental Health Act

As we have seen, although the word 'risk' is not within any of the statutory criteria for admission or for community orders, consideration of risk remains at the forefront of policy development and professional practice. Although this text cannot offer an in-depth analysis of risk in mental health services, the annual report of the *National Confidential Inquiry into Suicide and Homicide by People with Mental Illness* offers some interesting points. In their 2014 annual report, they noted:

> In our previous case control study on in-patient suicide, we found suicide to be linked to absconding and that use of the Mental Health Act was protective.

However, they also report that the rate of suicide in patients subject to CTOs is higher than the rate for all patients, and on that basis they cannot say whether CTOs have reduced the risk at this stage.

In their 2015 report, they report an 'increase in suicides of patients discharged from a non-local ward as well as in those under the care of Crisis & Home Treatment Teams', perhaps reflecting reduced availability of local in-patient beds, increasing reliance on home treatment as an alternative to admission and on beds that are out of the local area. Other important factors in suicide include the use of opiates, lack of involvement between family and services, and physical illness. Patients with a diagnosis of schizophrenia, often portrayed in the media as dangerous and violent, made up 216 deaths by suicide per year between 2003 and 2013 in England. Rates of alcohol or substance misuse in homicides by patients were 89 per cent in England and 93 per cent in Wales.

The National Confidential Inquiry into Suicides and Homicides by People with Mental Illness 2010 noted:

- Careful and effective care planning is needed on discharge including self-discharge.
- Early follow-up should be routine – suicide within three days of discharge should not happen.

- Adverse events that precede admission should have been addressed before discharge.
- The link to short admissions is a concern – the benefits of reducing length of in-patient stay should be balanced with risks, and it should not be an aim in itself.

Further reading

Burns et al. (2013) 'Community Treatment Orders for Patients with Psychosis (OCTET): A Randomised Controlled Trial.' The first comprehensive research piece on the efficacy of CTOs.

Department of Health (2007) *Best Practice in Managing Risk*. This document summarises current risk tools used in mental health. It also offers guidance on assessing risk in the context of mental health and involvement of service users.

Health and Social Care Information Centre (2014 and 2015) *In-patients Formally Detained in Hospitals under the MHA 1983 and Patients Subject to Supervised Community Treatment – Annual reports*.

University of Manchester (2015) *The National Confidential Inquiry into Suicide and Homicide by People with Mental Illness Annual Report 2015: England, Northern Ireland, Scotland and Wales*.

Stroud, J., K. Doughty and L. Banks (2013) *An Exploration of Service User and Practitioner Experiences of Community Treatment Orders*. This is a qualitative research piece emphasising service users' and carers' views of CTOs.

Welsh Government (2015) *Admission of Patients to Mental Health Facilities in Wales*. Includes revised statistics on the use of supervised community treatment (CTO).

5

PATIENTS CONCERNED IN CRIMINAL PROCEEDINGS OR UNDER SENTENCE

AT A GLANCE THIS CHAPTER COVERS:

- overview, terminology and professional roles
- arrest and diversion
- remand
- trial and defences
- sentencing and prison transfers
- further relevant statutory and policy provisions
- conditional discharge and social supervision

Overview, terminology and professional roles

The assessment and/or treatment of patients concerned in criminal proceedings is largely dealt with under Part III, MHA. This chapter, however, also considers other policy and legislation relevant to patients at each stage of contact with the criminal justice system, from the point of arrest to discharge from hospital following detention.

The Scheme of Part III is, on the face of it, relatively straightforward and, in summary, provides for the detention in hospital of patients: after charge; pre-sentencing; post conviction and for those already in prison either serving a custodial sentence or on remand. However, the interface with the criminal justice system and other statutory provisions and the nexus between treatment and punishment make this a legally and ethically complex area.

Terminology for this group of patients tends to be used interchangeably and sometimes misleadingly, and patients may be described as mentally disordered offenders or forensic patients ('forensic' simply meaning relating to the courts). However, it is perfectly possible for patients detained under one of the civil sections discussed in Chapter 3 to find themselves within forensic mental health services, even in conditions of high security, without having committed an offence. In addition, a patient may be detained or transferred from prison to hospital under Part III provisions before any conviction for an offence.

There is no equivalent in Part III to the AMHP role in civil detentions. Admissions and transfers are by order of the court or on the direction of the Secretary of State and founded on medical evidence. However, social workers are commonly found in multidisciplinary forensic mental health services, court diversion schemes, acting as appropriate adults under Police and Criminal Evidence Act 1984 (PACE) provisions or acting as social supervisor for conditionally discharged patients.

The safeguards discussed in Chapter 7 are heavily circumscribed for patients being dealt with under Part III provisions, particularly patients subject to restriction orders or limitation directions. The NR role is limited (in some cases, non-existent), and access to the MHT and the Tribunal's powers are also more limited for patients subject to Part III orders.

Although the legal mechanics for the diversion or transfer from prison exist, and despite a number of independent reviews discussed below recommending early intervention and diversion from the criminal justice system, the estimates for the prevalence of mental disorder within prisons make stark reading:

> It is estimated that 70% of the prison population have two or more diagnosed mental illnesses.
>
> (Edgar and Rickford 2009)

More specifically:

- 66% of prisoners have a personality disorder compared to 5% of the general population.
- 45% of prisoners have a mood disorder such as depression or anxiety compared to 14% of the general population (Centre for Mental Health, 2009).
- In 2013, 25% of women and 15% of men in prison reported symptoms indicative of psychosis (Ministry of Justice, 2013).
- The rate of psychosis in the general population is around 4% (Wiles et al. 2006). (McConnell and Talbot 2013)

Against this concerning background, it is also important to note that the powers to compulsorily treat mental disorder under the MHA do not extend to prisons (as a prison is not a hospital), giving rise to the potential for a seriously mentally ill person being detained in prison without access to appropriate medication or treatment. Such a position has been held by the ECtHR to be 'inhuman or degrading treatment or punishment' and therefore a breach of Article 3, ECHR (Hale 2010).

Arrest and diversion

Reference should be made to the police powers under s.136, MHA (discussed in Chapter 3), as this is a potential diversion from the criminal justice system to hospital at the earliest stage.

For those persons who are arrested for a criminal offence, there are a number of relevant legal and policy considerations.

There have been a number of Government-commissioned independent reviews of the provision of health and social care for mentally disordered offenders (e.g. *The Reed Report* [DH 1992]) and the issues facing persons in the criminal justice system with mental health issues or learning disabilities (e.g. *The Bradley Report* [DH 2009]). A common theme of these reviews was the need for early identification of mental health issues and diversion from the criminal justice system or signposting to appropriate treatment concurrent with the criminal proceedings. However, the overall picture was one of 'piecemeal and haphazard'

Table 5.1: Part III–Summary

Section	Decision-Maker	Evidence	Duration	Consent to Provision Treatments Apply (Part IV)?	Access to Mental Health Tribunal?	Nearest Relative Powers
S.35 – remand for reports	Magistrates' or Crown Court	One registered medical practitioner	28 days, renewable to max of 12 weeks	No	None	None
S.36 – remand for treatment	Crown Court	Two registered medical practitioners	28 days, renewable to max of 12 weeks	No	None	None
S.37 – hospital or order	Magistrates' or Crown Court	Two registered medical practitioners	Six months, renewable for six months and then annually	Yes	In 2nd six months and then each 12-month period	MHT applications as per patient
S.37 – guardianship order	Magistrates' or Crown Court	Two registered medical practitioners	Six months, renewable for six months then annually	No	In 1st six months, 2nd six months and then each 12-month period	MHT application in first 12 months and subsequent 12-month periods
S.38 – interim hospital order	Magistrates' or Crown Court	Two registered medical practitioners	12 weeks, renewable to max of 12 months	Yes	None	None
S.45A – hybrid order (hospital direction and limitation direction)	Crown Court	Two registered medical practitioners	Indeterminate	Yes	2nd six months and then in each 12-month period	None

S.47 – transfer of sentenced prisoner	Secretary of State	Two registered medical practitioners	Six months, renewable for six months, then annually	Yes	1st six months, 2nd six months, then in each 12-month period	None
S.48 – transfer of unsentenced prisoner	Secretary of State	Two registered medical practitioners	Six months, renewable for six months then annually	Yes	1st six months, 2nd six months, then in each 12-month period	None
S.37/41 – hospital order with restrictions	Crown Court	As for s.37 + oral evidence of at least one of the registered medical practitioners who provided the reports	Indeterminate	Yes	In 2nd six months and then in each 12-month period	None
s.47/49 – transfer of sentenced prisoner with restrictions	Secretary of State	As for s.47, no further evidence is required for the Secretary of State to add a restriction direction	Six months, renewable for six months, then annually	Yes	1st six months, 2nd six months, then in each 12-month period	None
S.48/49 – transfer of unsentenced prisoner with restrictions	Secretary of State	As for s.48, no further evidence is required for the Secretary of State to add a restriction direction	Six months, renewable for six months, then annually	Yes	1st six months, 2nd six months, then in each 12-month period	None

service development (Sainsbury Centre for Mental Health 2009). Work is continuing to harmonise these services with the development of the Liaison and Diversion Programme and a national service specification (NHS England 2014) for the provision of 'comprehensive and multi-disciplinary assessment of eligible referred individuals' from the initial entry point of a person being suspected of having committed a criminal offence. It is anticipated that a standardised service will have been rolled out to cover the whole of England by 2017–18.

Appropriate adults: Police and the Criminal Evidence Act 1984 (PACE)

PACE and its accompanying detailed Codes of Practice govern, among other things, police powers and duties, arrest and detention, and matters concerning evidence. PACE introduced the safeguard of the provision of an 'appropriate adult' for potentially vulnerable groups such as juveniles or the 'mentally vulnerable' or 'mentally incapable'. The relevant provisions are within PACE Code C, which deals with detention, treatment and questioning by police.

> If an officer has any suspicion, or is told in good faith, that a person of any age may be mentally disordered or otherwise mentally vulnerable, or mentally incapable of understanding the significance of questions or their replies that person shall be treated as mentally disordered or otherwise mentally vulnerable for the purposes of this Code.
>
> (para 1.4, Code C)

> If the custody officer authorises the detention of a person who is mentally vulnerable or appears to be suffering from a mental disorder, the custody officer must as soon as practicable inform the appropriate adult of the grounds for detention and the person's whereabouts, and ask the adult to come to the police station to see them.
>
> (para 3.15, Code C)

The 'appropriate adult' role can be undertaken by: a relative; guardian; other person responsible for the person's care or custody; someone experienced in dealing with mentally disordered or mentally vulnerable people but who is not a police officer or employed by the police (or in the absence of any of these groups, then any responsible adult not being a police officer or employee). However, PACE guidance goes on to say that:

> In the case of people who are mentally disordered or otherwise mentally vulnerable, it may be more satisfactory if the appropriate

adult is someone experienced or trained in their care rather than a relative lacking such qualifications.

(Note 1D, PACE Code C)

Therefore, it would not be at all unusual for a social worker to undertake this role.

Similarly to the issues with the diversion and liaison schemes discussed above, there is no statutory basis for the provision of appropriate adult schemes, and therefore their development and the availability of trained appropriate adults is geographically variable. Services may be operated directly by social services or subcontracted to the private or third sector (or not exist at all) (Perks 2010).

Once the need for an appropriate adult has been established, then a number of protective limits are placed on the actions that can be taken by the police. If a person has already been cautioned, then this must be repeated in the presence of the appropriate adult; the person must not be interviewed or asked to sign a statement in the absence of the appropriate adult; the appropriate adult must, if available, be present if the person is charged and be present for any searches, taking of samples, ID or fingerprinting procedures (there are some limited exceptions to all of these provisions which relate to urgency and the need to preserve evidence or manage risks).

In broad terms, the appropriate adult role is to provide support, advice and assistance to the detained person. It is to give procedural rather than legal advice, and it is important to note that the discussions between an appropriate adult and a detained person are not subject to the same legal privilege that protects solicitor/client discussions (legal privilege means that any communication between the client and his solicitor remains confidential and cannot be disclosed to a third party such as the police without the client's consent).

The appropriate adult has a number of rights such as to hear the grounds for detention, to view the custody record and notices of rights and entitlements provided to the detainee as well as to view the PACE Codes of Practice. The appropriate adult can request that a solicitor be called even if the detainee has refused legal advice.

Remand

Part III, MHA, contains provisions to enable the courts to remand an accused person to hospital at the pre-trial or pre-sentencing stage of criminal proceedings.

Where a mental disorder is suspected, s.35 MHA provides a power to remand to hospital for assessment (by way of a report to the court on the person's mental condition) and, where mental disorder has been established, s.36 MHA provides a power to remand to hospital for treatment.

These provisions could be used to assist the court in assessing fitness to plead (or to treat a mental disorder in the hope that fitness to plead might be recovered) or to assist the court at the stage of sentencing options being considered (particularly whether a hospital order might be appropriate).

An order under s.35 can be made by the Crown Court either before trial or before sentencing where the offence is one which could be punished with imprisonment; or by a magistrates' court either after conviction, where the court is satisfied that the person committed the offence or where the person consents to the remand and the offence is one which could be punished with imprisonment. The legal grounds for the order are that the court must have evidence from a registered medical practitioner (RMP) that there is reason to suspect the accused is suffering from mental disorder and that it would be impracticable for a report on the mental condition to be prepared while on bail.

The court must also have evidence from hospital managers or the clinician responsible for providing the report to the court that arrangements are in place for an admission to hospital within seven days. The order is initially for 28 days but can be renewed (for no more than 28-day periods) up to a maximum of 12 weeks. The consent to treatment provisions in Part IV MHA do not apply, and there is no power to compulsorily treat mental disorder. There is no right to apply to the Mental Health Tribunal, and the NR has no right to order discharge; indeed, neither the RC nor the hospital managers can discharge an order under this section.

The procedural matters and timescales for orders under s.36 are essentially the same as for s.35; the key difference is that only the Crown Court can make an order. The legal grounds are also different: the court must have evidence from two registered medical practitioners (one of whom must be approved under s.12, MHA) that the person is suffering from mental disorder of a nature or degree which makes it appropriate to be detained in hospital for medical treatment and that appropriate medical treatment is available (the wording is almost identical to the grounds for admission under section 3 – see Chapter 3).

Under both s.35 and s.36, the accused person has the right to obtain an independent report (at his own expense) on his mental condition in order to challenge the remand.

Trial and defences

Mental disorder may be relevant at the time of the offence, as it might give rise to possible defences. It may also be relevant at the point when the accused person is required to enter a plea to a charge.

Insanity

Surprisingly, the legal position in relation to raising a defence of insanity is still defined by a case from 1843, despite long-running academic criticism and continuing review of the issues of insanity and criminal responsibility. All of the defences and unfitness to plead matters discussed below are subject to long-running research, review and discussion (Law Commission 2013).

> **KEY CASE ANALYSIS**

M'Naghten's case [1843] UKHL J16

On 20 January 1843, Daniel M'Naghten shot and killed Edward Drummond (secretary to then Prime Minister, Sir Robert Peel). It has been suggested that M'Naghten may have believed he was shooting the Prime Minister. M'Naghten pleaded not guilty to the charge of murder on the basis that he was of unsound mind – specifically that he was labouring under a range of persecutory delusions concerning the Tories. M'Naghten was acquitted of the criminal charges and transferred initially to the Bethlem Hospital, later transferring to the newly opened Broadmoor Hospital.

However, following the conclusion of the criminal proceedings, the case led to debate in the House of Lords, and a series of abstract questions regarding insanity and criminal responsibility were referred to the Law Lords (what would now be a reference to the Supreme Court). The key response of the Law Lords, which remains the legal position today, was

[T]o establish a defence on the ground of insanity, it must be clearly proved that, at the time of the committing of the act, the party accused was labouring under such a defect of reason, from disease of the mind, as not to know the nature and quality of the act he was doing; or, if he did know it, that he did not know he was doing what was wrong.

In simple terms, the person must be shown to have either simply not known what he was doing at the time of the offence or, if he knew what he was doing, he did not know it was wrong. The presence of even a very severe mental illness, in itself, may not be sufficient to establish the defence of insanity. The widely cited examples that might meet this test are of a person who takes an axe to another person, believing that individual to be a block of wood (not knowing what he was doing) (Fennell, Letts and Wilson 2013), or the person who kills another person while believing himself to be God and therefore entitled to do so (not knowing it was wrong) (Hale 2010).

If the defence is successfully argued, then a special verdict of 'not guilty by reason of insanity' will be returned. The court then has only three sentencing options:

- A hospital order (with or without restrictions), the effect of which would be exactly as for a person convicted and sentenced to a hospital order (discussed below)
- A supervision order, which is a type of community order where the person will be under the supervision of either a probation officer or a social worker (usually an AMHP) for up to two years
- An absolute discharge, most likely for more minor offences where there is no finding that the person requires continuing treatment or supervision

For a range of complex reasons, the insanity defence is rarely used (Law Society 2013); not least that the defendant may prefer the option of a finite prison sentence to an indeterminate hospital admission:

> But which would you rather be? Sentenced to a fixed term in prison where there could be a stimulating range of educational and other opportunities available, smoking is allowed and forcible medical treatment can hardly ever be imposed? Or sentenced to an indeterminate term in a medium or high security psychiatric hospital, where the facilities are less varied, smoking is not allowed, but forcible medical treatment is?
>
> (Hale 2010)

Diminished responsibility

Diminished responsibility is a partial defence only available to a charge of murder. It could be raised as a defence even where the M'Naghten test is not met. If the plea is successful, the defendant will be found guilty of manslaughter on the grounds of diminished responsibility.

For a plea of diminished responsibility to succeed, the defence must satisfy the jury or the court that, at the time of the offence:

- The defendant was suffering from an abnormality of mental functioning arising from a recognised medical condition.
- The abnormality substantially impaired his ability to understand the nature of his conduct or form a rational judgement or exercise self-control.
- The abnormality caused or significantly contributed to the offence (paraphrased from s.52, Coroners and Justice Act 2009).

The origin of the plea was to mitigate cases where the death penalty might have applied. Essentially, the plea is an admission to the act, but because of the effects of a medical condition, the defendant should not be convicted of murder.

A conviction for manslaughter on the grounds of diminished responsibility would provide the court with a range of sentencing options such as imprisonment under criminal justice legislation or a hospital order (with or without restrictions), considered further below.

Infanticide

Similarly to diminished responsibility but in much more specific circumstances, s.1 Infanticide Act 1938 provides a partial defence to a charge of murder of a child under 12 months old for the child's mother where the 'balance of her mind was disturbed' due to the effects of birth or lactation. No direct causal link between the imbalance of the mind and the offence is required, and it is not necessary for any intent to be proven.

As with diminished responsibility, sentencing may be by way of a criminal justice disposal or a hospital order (with or without a restriction order), but a conviction for infanticide is likely to be treated more leniently and compassionately by the courts, and imprisonment is relatively unusual – as low as 6.1 per cent has been found in studies (McKay 2006, cited in Goslin et al. 2010).

Unfitness to plead

Whatever the defendant's mental state was at the time of the offence, it may be that, at the outset of criminal proceedings, the defendant is found to be unfit to plead. S.2, Criminal Procedure (Insanity and Unfitness to Plead) Act 1991 provides the statutory basis for such a finding:

> Finding of unfitness to plead.
> This section applies where on the trial of a person the question arises (at the instance of the defence or otherwise) whether the accused is under a disability, that is to say, under any disability such that apart from this Act it would constitute a bar to his being tried.

However, the test for unfitness to plead is not defined in statute and has developed from case law dating from 1836. Gostin et al. (2010) helpfully summarise the key issues from the complex case law that represent the test for unfitness as follows:

To be fit to plead, the defendant must be able to do *all* of the following:

- plead to the indictment (i.e. enter a plea of guilty or not guilty);
- understand the course of the proceedings;
- instruct a lawyer;
- challenge a juror; and
- understand the evidence.

The word 'fitness' in this context could easily be substituted with the word 'capacity', and one might wonder why the issue of being able to plead and to stand trial is not governed by the provisions of the MCA 2005. Indeed, this distinction has been subject to a great deal of academic criticism:

> It is astonishing, and possibly unlawful, that the civil law test for capacity and the criminal law test for unfitness to plead are contradictory. A person who would not have capacity, under the MCA, to take relatively trivial decisions about his life might be found fit to plead in the criminal law context and be expected to make such important decisions as to whether to plead guilty or not guilty or whether to give evidence in his own defence.
> (Scott-Moncrieff and Vassall-Adams 2006)

The issue of unfitness to plead can be raised by the defence, the prosecution, or the court, and the legal test is not confined to persons suffering from a mental disorder, so, for example, a person with significant communication difficulties for physical reasons could be found to be unfit.

A finding of unfitness will mean that a full trial cannot proceed, and instead the jury will consider a 'trial of the facts', essentially as good a trial as is practicable in light of the defendant's unfitness (s.2, Criminal Procedure (Insanity and Unfitness to Plead) Act 1991). The defendant could then be acquitted or, if the jury is satisfied beyond reasonable doubt, then a finding could be made that the defendant did the act or made the omission as charged. If such a finding (distinct from a conviction) is made, then the court's options are exactly as they are where a defendant is found not guilty by reason of insanity as detailed above. The court could also use its powers to remand the defendant (as discussed above) in order to obtain more information in respect of appropriate sentencing or to further assess the defendant's fitness to plead.

Sentencing and prison transfers

We have already seen that certain defences or a finding of unfitness to plead might lead to the court dealing with the defendant by way of a hospital order. In addition, following conviction, if the person is found to be suffering from mental disorder at the time of sentencing then the court has a number of non-penal disposals available (see grid above).

Restriction and hybrid orders

Section 37, MHA, provides the Crown or magistrates' courts with the power to order admission to hospital or guardianship. The offence must be one which would be punishable with imprisonment. For more serious offences or where the offender is considered high risk, hospital orders under this section may also be made alongside a restriction order, considered further below.

However, the legal criteria, timescales, effect and implications for the patient of a s.37 order (without a restriction order) are almost exactly the same as they would be for a patient detained under s.3, MHA, or received into guardianship under s.7, MHA. There is no continuing involvement of the court or the Secretary of State, and the purpose is entirely to provide medical treatment rather than to punish (*R v Birch* [1989]). As with the civil sections, the orders are initially for six months and then renewable for 6-month and then 12-month periods.

In summary, the legal grounds for a s.37 hospital order are that the offender is suffering from a mental disorder of a nature or degree that makes it appropriate for him to be detained in hospital for medical treatment, and appropriate treatment is available to him or, in the case of a guardianship order, the offender is suffering from a mental disorder of a nature or degree which warrants his reception into guardianship. Unlike the civil provisions for admission under s.3, the court does not have to be satisfied that detention for medical treatment is necessary in the interests of the patient's health or their safety, or for the protection of others, and similarly, unlike the civil provisions for reception into guardianship under s.7, the court does not need to be satisfied that it is in the interests of the welfare of the patient or for the protection of others that he or she is received into guardianship. However, there is a general criteria that the order is the most suitable disposal in all the circumstances.

An s.37 order must be founded on the evidence of two registered medical practitioners, and the court must also have evidence from the clinician who would be responsible for the offender's case or a representative of the hospital managers that arrangements for the admission within 28 days are in place.

Patients subject to s.37 hospital orders do not have a right to apply to the Mental Health Tribunal until the second six months of the order, and the patient's NR has no power to order discharge under s.23, although the NR can also apply to the Tribunal at any point when the patient would be eligible (see Chapter 7).

Part IV MHA consent to treatment provisions apply to hospital order patients, though not to s.37 guardianship patients.

Interim hospital orders

Despite the remand powers already considered, it may be that uncertainty remains as to whether a hospital order is an appropriate disposal for an offender. Questions may remain regarding the existence of a mental disorder, whether the disorder is amenable to treatment or whether the offender will cooperate with treatment. In these circumstances, s.38 MHA gives the court the option of making an interim hospital order in order to establish whether a hospital order ought to be the final disposal. The procedural requirements are largely the same as for s.37 orders. Interim orders are made for an initial period of 12 weeks and can be renewed in 28-day periods up to a maximum of 12 months. At any stage, the court can decide to make a full hospital order or deal with the matter in another way (e.g. a prison sentence) on the evidence of the RC.

There is no access to the Mental Health Tribunal, and there is no NR power to order discharge or right to apply to the Tribunal. The consent to treatment provisions of Part IV MHA apply, and the order can only be ended by the court.

Restriction orders

S.41, MHA, empowers the Crown Court, when making a hospital order, to attach further restrictions on the offender's management by way of a restriction order in cases where due to the nature of the offence, history of offending and risk of reoffending if at large, it is necessary for the protection of the public from serious harm.

The effects of a restriction order are far reaching and 'severe' (Hale 2010) and essentially mean that any key decisions in the patient's further management while in hospital and beyond are restricted by the continued involvement of the Secretary of State (in practice, this is undertaken by the Mental Health Casework Section of the Ministry of Justice). The summary of the effects of a restriction order, below, are adapted from the Reference Guide to the Mental Health Act 1983 in chapter 21:

- Responsible clinicians may only grant leave of absence from hospital with the consent of the Secretary of State. The Secretary of State may recall patients from leave of absence at any time. This is in addition to the power of responsible clinicians to recall patients from leave.
- Restricted patients may not be discharged onto a CTO, but may be conditionally discharged.
- There is no time limit after which the patient may no longer be taken into custody and returned to hospital or any other place the patient ought to be if absent without leave.
- Hospital managers may only transfer patients from one hospital to another with the consent of the Secretary of State.
- The order is indefinite. The authority to detain does not expire, so no renewal is required. The authority to detain does not expire, no matter how long the patient is absent without leave.
- The responsible clinician and hospital managers may only discharge patients with the consent of the Secretary of State.
- Restricted patients do not have a nearest relative for the purposes of the Act.
- The patient may not apply to the Tribunal until the expiry of six months.

- Hospital managers' duty to refer to the Tribunal does not apply, but the Secretary of State has a duty to refer patients if they have not had a hearing for three years (one year if under age 18).
- The Tribunal has no discretionary power to discharge and no power to make statutory recommendations in respect of leave or transfer.

'Hybrid orders'

The Crime (Sentences) Act 1997 introduced s.45A into the MHA – a new power for the court to direct admission to hospital with a limitation direction (the effect of which is the same as a restriction order as above). The term 'hybrid order' has been coined, as these orders are made concurrently with a prison sentence.

The purpose of the new power was to provide a disposal for offenders who may be suffering from a mental disorder but nevertheless retained a higher degree of responsibility for their offence or where treatment for mental disorder could be tested out and, if unsuccessful, then the offender could be returned to prison. The orders have been rarely used (in 2013, there were 46 patients in hospital under s.45A out of a total of 4449 detained restricted patients), and doubt has been expressed as to whether s.45A fulfils any purpose that could not have been achieved with the existing Part III powers available to the court or the Secretary of State (Peay 2015).

Procedural matters such as access to the Tribunal are the same as for a restriction order.

Transfers from prison

The final powers within Part III to consider are the provisions dealing with the transfer of prisoners (s.47 deals with sentenced prisoners and s.48 deals with unsentenced prisoners – primarily those on remand). Decisions regarding transfer are made by the Secretary of State, rather than the court, and founded on reports from two registered medical practitioners. The legal grounds are exactly as for hospital orders, as detailed above, and the consent to treatment provisions under Part IV MHA apply.

In the vast majority of cases, transfer orders will be made with a restriction order under s.49 MHA. Broadly, the position of a patient transferred without a restriction order is the same as that of a patient detained under a hospital order, and the position of a patient transferred with a restriction order is the same as that of a restricted hospital order patient.

For patients transferred under s.47 or s.49 without a restriction order, the position in respect of eligibility to apply to the Tribunal is slightly different to those patients detained as a result of a court order; as the transfer does not follow from a consideration of the patient's case by a court, the patient can apply to the Tribunal within the first six months of detention.

For patients detained under these transfer provisions (with restrictions) and also for patients detained under s.45A, there is a more limited role for the Mental Health Tribunal. Although patients under any of these provisions will be eligible to apply to the Tribunal in the first six months, the Tribunal does not have the power to discharge – this decision remains with the Secretary of State. If the Tribunal finds that were the patient subject to a hospital order with restrictions he would be entitled to an absolute or conditional discharge, the Tribunal must notify the Secretary of State. It is then for the Secretary of State to make decisions regarding whether the patient should receive an absolute or conditional discharge, remain in hospital or return to prison (s.74 MHA). The issue for this group of patients is that there is either an underlying or concurrent prison sentence. However, the restrictions will end when the earliest date of release (had they remained in prison) passes. At this stage, if still detained in hospital, the patient will become what is known as a 'notional s.37' patient, and the position in relation to Tribunal applications and powers is exactly as it would be for a patient subject to a s.37 hospital order.

PRACTICE FOCUS

Iris

Iris is a 40-year-old woman who lives alone in a small flat in south-east London. Police are called to a busy high street by members of the public late on a Saturday evening as Iris has been observed in an agitated and distressed state, walking in and out of the very busy road and appearing to be trying to direct fast-moving traffic. Police officers attempt to speak with Iris and to persuade her to return from the middle of the road to the pavement. Iris becomes increasingly hostile and threatening, and officers, fearing for her immediate safety, attempt to physically escort her out of the road. Iris lashes out, causing minor injuries to one of the officers. She is arrested and taken to the local police station.

In custody, Iris appears anxious, fearful and is uncooperative – she refuses the offer of seeing a solicitor. She is interviewed and charged with assault on a police officer and a number of public order offences. She is granted bail and returns home. However, the following day, Iris is involved in a further incident in a high street shop, resulting in her throwing a can and smashing the front shop window. She is arrested again and on this occasion presents as mute – again refusing any legal advice. Police view her as being deliberately uncooperative, and she is charged with further criminal damage offences. On this occasion, she is refused bail and held in custody pending appearance at the local magistrates' court.

Iris pleads guilty to all of the charges. At court she presents as flippant, unconcerned and distracted – infuriating the magistrates, who impose a custodial sentence. Iris is subsequently transferred to prison.

Over the course of the next few weeks, prison staff become increasingly concerned regarding Iris' presentation. She is isolative, sleeping and eating very little, and there are several episodes of her self-harming by cutting, scratching and banging her head. Iris is transferred to the hospital wing of the prison for further assessment.

- Question: At what stages could (or should) Iris have been diverted from the criminal justice system to the mental health system?

Further relevant statutory and policy provisions

Multi Agency Public Protection Arrangements (MAPPA)

The Ministry of Justice MAPPA Guidance (2012) summarises the purpose of the arrangements:

> These are designed to protect the public, including previous victims of crime, from serious harm by sexual and violent offenders. They require the local criminal justice agencies and other bodies dealing with offenders to work together in partnership in dealing with these offenders.

Three categories of offenders would be eligible for MAPPA: registered sexual offenders; violent and other sexual offenders; and other dangerous offenders. Offenders are then managed at one of three levels of intervention depending on the level of risk posed to the public.

Patients subject to Part III orders may well be referred to MAPPA.

The significance of MAPPA involvement for a patient may take a number of forms, particularly in relation to Tribunal proceedings:

- The social circumstances report prepared by the detaining authority for the Tribunal must include details of any MAPPA involvement along with contact details of the MAPPA meeting chairperson and the representative of the lead agency.
- If MAPPA wishes to submit views to the Tribunal, then this may be appended to the social circumstances report along with any details of previous convictions.
- S.325, Criminal Justice Act 2003, places a duty on health services dealing with mentally disordered offenders who may be MAPPA eligible to cooperate with MAPPA in the assessment and management of such patients. This may include referral to MAPPA and notifications at certain trigger points such as when unescorted leave is being considered or when plans are being made towards discharge from hospital.

MAPPA has recently introduced a website for professionals and members of the public; the link is included in the Further reading list below.

Domestic Violence, Crime and Victims Act 2004 (DVCVA)

The DCVCA brought in a range of victims' rights (and in some cases rights for victims' families) in relation to decisions regarding offender management, and these rights apply equally to restricted and (since the 2007 MHA amendments) unrestricted hospital order patients as well as some categories of patients transferred from prison. An extensive list of offences triggers these rights, but essentially they apply in cases of violent or sexual offences. The Act applies to patients sentenced on or after 1 July 2005 for restricted patients, and for non-restricted patients, after 3 November 2008.

In summary, the victims' rights relate to the receipt of information and to make representations.

This right extends to Tribunal proceedings, and victims have a statutory right to make representations limited to the questions of whether, if discharged, any conditions should be imposed and, if so, what those conditions should be.

Liaison between the victims and the various agencies involved is via victim liaison officers within the Probation Service for restricted patients and via the hospital managers for unrestricted patients.

The victim's representations would ordinarily be in writing, although a request to attend a hearing in person will be considered by the Tribunal and a decision made on the basis of whether attendance in person is required in order for the case to be dealt with fairly and justly.

Conditional discharge and social supervision

As stated, unlike civil admissions to hospital, the social work role is much more limited in relation to patients concerned in criminal proceedings, and there is no equivalent of the statutory AMHP role. However, the social supervision of conditionally discharged restricted patients merits consideration, as this is a role that will commonly be carried out by AMHPs or social workers.

It is very rare for restricted patients to receive an absolute discharge directly from hospital, only reaching double figures on two occasions since 2004 (Bartlett and Sandland 2013). It is much more usual for restricted patients to receive a conditional discharge in the first instance, either granted by the MHT (s.73(2) MHA 1983) or the Secretary of State (42(3) MHA 1983) (technically, the RC or the hospital managers can discharge a restricted patient, but as this still requires the consent of the Secretary of State, it is only a notional power (Sch I, Part II MHA 1983).

Conditional discharge is exactly as it sounds: the patient is released from detention in hospital subject to conditions imposed either by the Tribunal or the Secretary of State. Conditions cover matters such as place of residence, to comply with treatment and to submit to clinical and social supervision by mental health services. The Secretary of State retains a power to recall the patient to hospital until such time that the patient is granted an absolute discharge (s.42(3) MHA 1983).

Although not defined in statute, conditions inevitably include requirements to comply with social and clinical supervision, and the Ministry of Justice has, as a matter of policy, detailed requirements for the social supervision of conditionally discharged restricted patients, requiring the concerned professionals to provide regular written reports to the Secretary of State on the patient's progress in the community and to notify of any significant changes in the care plan or personnel dealing with the case. Any changes (such as change of address) that would require an amendment to the original conditions of discharge require notification and the agreement of the Ministry of Justice.

On-the-spot question — Why is it necessary to update the Secretary of State on any significant changes in the care plan of a conditionally discharged restricted patient?

Following two high-profile homicides, *The Independent Inquiry into the Care and Treatment of Peter Bryan* (NHS England 2009) made a number of recommendations regarding the training and experience requirements for professionals dealing with mentally disordered offenders in the community, and specifically:

> The Ministry of Justice should revise their Guidance to Social Supervisors to include a requirement that local authority Social Supervisors should be Mental Health Approved Social Workers (ASWs) as a minimum requirement and where possible should have at least two years experience as an ASW.
>
> (NB: The ASW has now been replaced by the Approved Mental Health Professional [AMHP])

The Ministry of Justice *Guidance for Social Supervisors* (2009) does not specify which professions may undertake the social supervision role; however, the Reference Guide to the MHA refers to social supervision from 'a social worker, AMHP or Probation Officer' (para 27.38).

The Code of Practice goes further by stating at para 22.80 that social supervisors 'shall be allocated by local authorities, who will determine that their agreed social supervisors have the correct knowledge, expertise and skills to undertake this role in line with the efficiency and equity principle'. It remains to be seen how this is applied in practice, particularly in disaggregated mental health services where social workers may no longer be the CPA care coordinator or integrated with health colleagues.

Further guidance on patients concerned with criminal proceedings can be found in chapter 22, MHA Code of Practice.

Further reading

Books

Law Commission (2013) *Criminal Liability: Insanity and Automatism. A Discussion Paper*. Detailed discussion of the defences discussed in this chapter.

Ministry of Justice (2015) *Guidance for Working with MAPPA and Mentally Disordered Offenders*. Detailed guidance on the roles and responsibilities within MAPPA arrangements. Further information for the public and professionals at mappa.justice.gov.uk.

Website

www.appropriateadult.org.uk. Organisation specifically for practitioners acting as appropriate adults, with a vast amount of relevant information and guidance.

6

TREATMENT AND CONSENT

Legal principles and definitions

The very first sentence of the MHA says: 'The provisions of this Act shall have effect with respect of the reception, care and treatment of mentally disordered patients' (s.1(1) MHA 1983). Despite the enormous complexity of mental health legislation, in essence, the MHA is a legal framework to ensure that people with mental disorder can be treated without their consent if necessary. A legal framework is required because, ordinarily, medical treatment without consent may be both a trespass against the person under the civil law and an assault under the criminal law (*Sidaway v Board of Governors of the Bethlem Royal Hospital* [1985]).

Clearly, medical treatment decisions in relation to a person subject to compulsion under the MHA will largely be the domain of the RC and medical staff. However, it is important for social workers acting as care coordinators or AMHPs to have knowledge of the legal framework regarding consent to treatment in order that clients (and families) can be properly informed about what can or cannot be imposed on a patient under the MHA.

The Code defines valid consent in general as

> agreeing to allow someone else to do something to you or for you. Particularly consent to treatment. Valid consent requires that the person has the capacity to make the decision (or the competence to consent if a child) and they are given the information they need to make the decisions and that they are not under any duress or inappropriate pressure.
>
> (Annex A)

In relation to medical treatment the Code defines consent as

> the voluntary and continuing permission of a patient to be given a particular treatment, based on a sufficient knowledge of the purpose, nature, likely effects and risks of that treatment, including the likelihood of its success and any alternatives to it. Permission given under any unfair or undue pressure is not consent.
>
> (para 24.34)

The single most important factor in understanding consent to treatment is that although good practice indicates that consent should always be sought, it is not a condition of giving the treatment. Treatment can be *imposed* upon someone with a mental disorder under MHA provisions.

Not all of the provisions for admission or compulsion in the community allow for treatment to be imposed at all. Broadly, the short-term powers (s.4, s.5, s.135, s.136) do not permit treatment without the patient's consent. In addition, patients remanded by the courts under s.35 or s.36 cannot be given treatment without consent. Finally, there is no power to compulsorily treat conditionally discharged restricted (s.37/41) patients (although the threat of recall by the Secretary of State could be seen as de facto compulsion) or patients subject to guardianship orders (s.7 and s.37). The position for patients subject to CTOs is considered separately below. The categories of patients to whom Part IV does or does not apply is set out in s.56 MHA.

Part IV refers to treatment for *mental* disorder, not physical disorders. However, it could include the treatment of symptoms or consequences of a mental disorder. In *B v Croydon Health Authority* [1995], a woman with borderline personality disorder was refusing to eat as a form of self-harm. Feeding by nasogastric tube was held to be treatment for a mental disorder as it was treatment for a symptom of the mental disorder, and to prevent deterioration and alleviate the consequences of the disorder. Jones (2015) refers to blood testing for the monitoring of a patient being treated with Clozapine as within the definition of treatment for a mental disorder. A blood transfusion may also be within the definition (*Nottinghamshire Healthcare NHS Trust v RC* [2014]). However, see Chapter 8 for more discussion on advance decisions to refuse treatment. Medical professions need to consider whether the physical disorder is connected to the mental disorder before relying on Part IV.

Medical treatment is given a wide definition in s.145 and includes

> nursing, psychological intervention and specialist mental health habilitation, rehabilitation and care ... the purpose of which is to alleviate, or prevent the worsening of, the disorder or one or more of its symptoms or manifestations.

In addition, for a number of provisions under the MHA there is an additional requirement that 'appropriate treatment' is be available to the patient (s.3, s.17A, s.36, s.37, s.45A, s.47, s.48), which is further defined as

> medical treatment which is appropriate in his case, taking into account the nature and degree of the mental disorder and all other circumstances of his case.
>
> (s.3(4))

As we saw in the introduction, these definitions were introduced, with some controversy, in the 2007 MHA amendments.

Although mere containment without treatment would be unlawful (*MD v Nottinghamshire Health Care NHS Trust* [2010]), Jones (2015) makes the point that both the current test for appropriate treatment and the court's very inclusive approach to the previous treatability test are 'so broad that it is difficult to imagine the circumstances that would cause a patient to fail it'. For all the controversy and debate around the 2007 amendment, it could be argued that the position for the detained patient changed very little.

There have been a number of unsuccessful challenges on the issue of whether appropriate treatment is available, which have established the following points of law:

The patient's refusal to receive a treatment does not mean it is not available or appropriate (*SH v Cornwall* [2012]).

- It is enough that the treatment manages the patient's environment to reduce conflict; it is not necessary for the treatment to address the core disorder or to provide new skills to the patient (*re Ian Brady* [2013]).
- The ward *milieu* in itself may amount to appropriate treatment (*MD v Nottinghamshire* [2010]) – see below.

→ **KEY CASE ANALYSIS** ←

MD v Nottinghamshire Health Care NHS Trust [2010] UKUT 59 (AAC)

Following conviction for a number of serious violent offences, MD was transferred to Rampton High Security Hospital in 2006 under s.47/49 MHA having been diagnosed as suffering from a psychopathic personality disorder. He remained detained beyond what would have been his release date from prison. In the view of the hospital, MD's psychological defence mechanisms prevented him from engaging with any formal therapy. After an unsuccessful application to the Mental Health Tribunal, MD appealed to the Upper-tier Tribunal on the basis that appropriate treatment was not available to him and therefore the Mental Health Tribunal had made an error of law by not discharging him from detention.

The Upper-tier Tribunal, in dismissing the appeal, held the following in relation to appropriate treatment:

- It is not necessary for treatment to reduce the risks posed by the patient in order for it to be appropriate treatment.
- The patient may benefit from the ward milieu in the short and long term; therefore, his detention was not mere containment.
- The boundary between treatment and confinement is a matter of fact and judgement for the Tribunal.

The drafting of Part IV MHA is complex. However, the underlying principle is really very straightforward: in essence, the more serious or invasive the treatment proposed, the greater the level of safeguards that are required before the treatment can be given to a patient subject to compulsory powers under the MHA.

It is important to note the way in which Part IV is structured. It would be easy to misread this part as being an inclusive list of treatments that can be provided to patients subject to compulsory powers. In fact, any treatment for mental disorder that is not explicitly covered by ss.57, 58 and 58A (see below) can be given without consent (s.63 MHA).

This part of the MHA makes frequent reference to requirements for certification by a doctor other than the AC in charge of the patient's treatment – that is, a second opinion. In practice, these are provided by second opinion appointed doctors (SOADs) appointed by the CQC. Practitioners may hear patients being described as 'T2 'or 'T3' patients. This is simply a reference to the type of certificate under which medical treatment is being provided. If the patient consents and has capacity, then a T2 certificate is completed; if the patient does not consent or lacks the capacity to consent, then a T3 certificate is completed.

Neurosurgery (s.57)

These treatments are defined as 'any surgical operation for destroying brain tissue or for destroying the functioning of brain tissue'. S.57 also provides for other treatments to be included if specified in regulations by the Secretary of State – presumably to allow any new treatments of similar gravity to be covered. These treatments, unsurprisingly, have the highest level of legal safeguards attached to them, not least as the procedures are irreversible.

The term 'psychosurgery' is often used to describe these treatments, and they are rarely used: the most recent CQC data shows that that only seven such treatments have been certified since 2009 (CQC 2015b).

The safeguards in s.57 apply to all patients, including informal patients (s.56(1) MHA):

- The patient's consent is required irrespective of legal status.
- A panel of three CQC representatives (which must include a SOAD) has certified that the patient understands the nature, purpose and likely effects of the treatment and has consented to it.
- The SOAD must additionally certify that it is appropriate for the treatment to be given.
- Therefore, save for urgent situations (considered below), there are no circumstances when these treatments could be imposed on a patient and no circumstances where a patient lacking the capacity to give consent could be given this treatment.

Medication (s.58)

S.58, which only applies to detained patients, provides additional safeguards when it is proposed to give a patient medication for a period exceeding three months. It covers any medicine administered in any form if it is treatment for a mental disorder – commonly, this would include anti-psychotics, mood stabilisers, anti-depressants or anti-anxiety medications.

The three-month period runs from when treatment starts and is not affected by a change in a detained patient's legal status – for example, if a patient is admitted under s.2 and then further detained under s.3.

The s.58 safeguards are as follows:

- Treatment cannot be provided unless the patient consents and either the AC in charge of the patient's treatment or a SOAD has certified that the patient understands the nature, purpose and likely effects of the treatment and has consented to it.
- If the patient does not consent or lacks capacity to consent, then treatment cannot be provided unless a SOAD has certified as to the lack of consent or the lack of capacity to consent; and, in the course of

making a decision as to whether to complete a certificate, the SOAD must consult with a nurse and another professional concerned with the patient's treatment – such as a social worker.

- Therefore, save for urgent situations, treatment under s.58 cannot be provided unless the patient consents or the relevant SOAD certificate is obtained.

> **PRACTICE FOCUS**
>
> Neive was admitted to hospital for assessment of an eating disorder on s.2 and has now been on s.3 for a month. The RC considers that she understands and has consented to treatment for anorexia. However, recently Neive's weight has dropped, and she is now refusing further treatment.
>
> - What steps should the RC take before imposing any treatment on Neive for the anorexia?

Electro-convulsive therapy (ECT) (s.58A)

ECT has tended to provoke extreme and divided opinion, and images of forcible 'shock treatment' endure in popular culture. For a helpful and concise summary of the history and operation of ECT, the Royal College of Psychiatrists information leaflet referenced at the end of the chapter is a useful starting point. Use of ECT has steadily declined since the 1980s (Stein and Wilkinson 2007), and the National Institute for Health and Care Excellence now recommends ECT only in cases of severe depression, catatonia or severe mania (NICE 2003).

The emotive nature of this treatment was recognised by Parliament during the passage of the 2007 amendments and resulted in s.58A being inserted into the MHA – adding an additional safeguard in that capacitated patients can no longer be treated without their consent.

The s.58A safeguards are as follows:

- For a patient over the age of 18, the patient must consent, and either the AC in charge of the patients' treatment or a SOAD has certified that the patient understands the nature, purpose and likely effects of the treatment and has consented to it.
- For a patient that lacks capacity, a SOAD must certify: that the patient does *not* understand the nature, purpose and likely effects of the

treatment; that it is appropriate for the treatment to be given; and that providing the treatment would not be in conflict with an advance decision or decision by a donee or deputy under the MCA.

- In the course of making a decision as to whether to complete a certificate, the SOAD must consult with a nurse and another professional concerned with the patient's treatment – such as a social worker.
- Again, the safeguards may not apply in urgent situations.

On-the-spot question

Treatment has not alleviated Aggie's chronic depression, and she is now unable to eat, drink or communicate. A decision has been made to treat her with ECT. What are the relevant safeguards for this proposed treatment?

Urgent treatment (s.62)

Despite the detailed procedural safeguards for treatments under s.57, s.58 and s.58A, the MHA does permit urgent treatment that is immediately necessary to be provided without complying with the safeguards. A common example would be where there is a delay in securing the necessary SOAD certificate, and there is an urgent need to continue with medication.

There is, however, a strict threshold for the justification of urgent treatment under s.62. For neurosurgery or medication beyond three months, such treatment must be one of the following:

- immediately necessary to save the patient's life;
- (not being irreversible) is immediately necessary to prevent a serious deterioration of his condition;
- (not being irreversible or hazardous) is immediately necessary to alleviate serious suffering by the patient;
- (not being irreversible or hazardous) is immediately necessary and represents the minimum interference necessary to prevent the patient from behaving violently or being a danger to himself or to others.

For ECT, urgent treatment must be one of the following:

- immediately necessary to save the patient's life; or
- (not being irreversible) is immediately necessary to prevent a serious deterioration of his condition.

Community treatment orders (CTOs)

The 2007 amendments introduced Part 4A to the MHA concerning patients in the community under CTOs.

The provisions in relation to CTOs are complex, largely due to the complications that can arise in relation to the certification of treatment when a patient may have moved from being detained in hospital to being in the community on a CTO and then perhaps being recalled. Perhaps the most important issue to be aware of is that, contrary to popular belief, it is not possible for persons subject to a CTO to be treated against their will in the community. Consideration of the grounds for recall may become relevant in such situations (see below). The Code summarises the position for CTO patients at paras 24.14–24.55.

As Chapter 4 clarifies, patients can move between being subject to a CTO in the community, being recalled to a hospital or having their CTO revoked.

There are certification requirements at various stages in this process and particular rules for child patients.

While subject to a CTO and not recalled, Part 4A applies. Treatment for mental disorder can only be given to adult patients with capacity to consent. Where such patients refuse, treatment cannot be imposed. Recall may have to be considered but refusal alone would not be grounds for recall.

Where adult patients lack capacity to consent, treatment can be given if the patient does not object. Treatment can also be given to patients lacking capacity in an emergency, using force if necessary. Where patients have fluctuating capacity, their capacity to consent to treatment should be regularly assessed by the clinician in charge.

For patients under 16 years there are specific requirements for the assessment of competence to consent to treatment and certification of that treatment. There are provisions for treatment in emergencies that mirror those above for adult patients. Those with parental responsibility cannot consent on behalf of a child patient on a CTO.

Recalls and revocations (s.62A)

S.62A deals with CTO patients following recall to hospital under s.17E or where the CTO has been revoked under s.17F. In both cases, Part IV applies, and subject to the certification complexities, their situation is largely as for other patients subject to Part IV.

Children

In relation to ECT, there are further Part IV provisions specifically in relation to children or young people, whether they are detained or not.

- For ECT to be given to a patient under the age of 18, the patient's consent is required along with SOAD certification that the patient has consented and is capable of understanding the nature, purpose and likely effects of the treatment; and that it is appropriate for the treatment to be given.
- If the patient lacks the capacity to consent, then SOAD certification is required that the patient is not capable of understanding the nature, purpose and likely effects of the treatment and that it is appropriate for the treatment to be given; for a 16- to 17-year-old, the decision is not in conflict with any decision made by the Court of Protection or a deputy appointed by the Court of Protection.
- The provisions of s.58A apply to patients under 18, whether they are subject to compulsory powers under the MHA or not (s.56(5)). However, for an informal patient under the age of 16 lacking Gillick competence to consent, or for a 16- to 17-year-old patient lacking capacity to consent, further authority to provide ECT is required (s.56(5)) – for under 16s this might be parental consent; for 16- to 17-year-olds, this might be reliance on s.5 MCA (see Chapter 8).

Further reading

Book

Brown, R., P. Barber and D. Martin (2009) *The Approved Mental Health Professional's Guide to Psychiatry and Medication.* Helpful guide for non-medical professionals on common disorders and treatments.

Websites

www.mind.org.uk/ Mind explains common questions about consent and treatment for mental disorder.

www.rcpsych.ac.uk/healthadvice/treatmentswellbeing/ect.aspx. Royal College of Psychiatrists – Information about ECT.

7

SAFEGUARDS

AT A GLANCE THIS CHAPTER COVERS:

- the nearest relative
- the Mental Health Tribunal
- hospital managers
- the Care Quality Commission and Health Inspectorate Wales

This chapter explores the main safeguards against arbitrary detention and the role of inspection services. The nearest relative (NR), Mental Health Tribunal (MHT) and hospital managers all have powers to discharge patients from detention.

The nearest relative

Relatives have played a role in admission and detention of family members for many years. The Madhouses Act 1774 introduced 'certification' by a relative of a 'lunatic'. The 1959 MHA introduced the current hierarchy of relatives referred to below in s.26.

The NR is a concept unique to the MHA and is not the same as 'next of kin'. NRs have specific powers and rights that provide some potentially powerful safeguards of the patient's A5 right to liberty. However, these powers do not apply to patients subject to short-term detention (such as s.135, s.136 or s.5) or patients detained under Part III court orders or transfer directions. The NR's powers and rights are as follows:

- They can make applications (s.11(1)) for assessment, treatment and Guardianship (s.2, s.4, s.3 and s.7).
- They can require the local authority to arrange for an AMHP to 'consider the patient's case' for possible admission under s.2 or s.3 and provide a reason in writing if they do not do so (s.13(4)).
- No application can be made for s.3 or s.7 without first consulting with them (unless it would involve 'unreasonable delay' or is 'not reasonably practicable').
- They must be informed of an application for admission under s.2 (s.11(3)).
- They can order the discharge of their relative from certain sections under section 23, giving 72 hours' notice of their intention to the hospital managers (although there are limitations on this, which we look at later in this chapter).
- They can instruct an independent doctor or AC to visit the patient and inspect records in order to advise on a possible NR order for discharge, as above (s.24(1) and (2)).
- In certain circumstances, they can apply to the MHT, and hospital managers are obliged to tell them of this right and their other rights (s.132(4), s.66(1)(ii)).

- They can request an IMHA visit their relative (s.130B(5)(a)).
- They should be informed of the discharge of their relative (from detention or a CTO), at least seven days before discharge, where practicable (s.133(1)), unless the patient has requested that this information should not be given (s.133(2)).
- They can delegate their role (Regulation 24 [England] or Regulation 33 [Wales]).

Identification of relatives and the nearest relative

S.26 starts out by providing a hierarchical list of 'relatives' within the meaning of the Act. There is no lower age limit for 'relatives' as this only applies when looking at the 'nearest relative'. The AMHP should 'have regard to any wishes expressed by relatives of the patient' (s.13(1)(b)), which could include young people and children, whose views might be overlooked. The s.26 list is as follows:

- husband or wife (or civil partner or marital partner of a same-sex couple)
- son or daughter
- father or mother
- brother or sister
- grandparents
- grandchildren
- uncle or aunt
- nephew or niece

S.26 does not favour one gender over the other, although the list may give that impression.

S.26(3) then explains that the 'nearest' relative will usually be the person at the top of the list above.

There are, however, some additional rules around establishing the NR, making the AMHP's job complex at times. Section 11(3) states that the AMHP will take such reasonable steps as are practicable to inform the person (if any) *appearing to be the nearest relative*. The court will not interfere with the AMHP's identification unless the AMHP has failed to apply the test in s.26 or acted in bad faith or reached a conclusion that was plainly wrong (*Re: D (Mental Patient: Habeas Corpus)* [2000]). The main rules for identification of the nearest relative are set out as follows:

- Whole blood are preferred to half blood (but note that the relative must be a blood relative and cannot be included if a step-parent or step-sibling. Adopted children are treated as the blood children of their parents (s.46(2) Adoption and Children Act 2002).

- Elder are preferred to younger persons if there are two people on the same point of the hierarchy, for example son and daughter.
- Controversially, s.26(2) refers to 'illegitimate' children being the legitimate child of their mother but only of the father if he holds parental responsibility (PR) (s.3(1) Children Act 1989). This has led to debate about the position for over 18s when PR has ended and there exists the potential discrimination of ruling out fathers and their families from the list, depending on the interpretation taken of s.26(2) (Hale 2010; Jones 2014; Bartlett and Sandland 2014; Hewitt 2013).
- Those who have divorced or permanently separated are excluded from being NR. If co-habiting in an intimate relationship, this must be for no less than six months before a person can be considered, but certain additional rules apply where one party remains married to someone else.
- NRs must be 18 or over unless they are married to the patient or in a civil partnership with them (see s.26(5)(c)).
- Relatives must live in the British Isles (Interpretation Act 1978, s.5, Sch 1) if the patient does and cannot be considered NR otherwise (s.26(5)(a)). This is probably as a result of the requirement for NRs to be able to use their powers and rights, which may prove difficult if they reside abroad. If, however, the patient does not reside in the British Isles (e.g. perhaps is on holiday here), then their relatives need not either.

Ordinarily residing with or caring for. Should anyone on the list above be 'ordinarily residing with' or 'caring for' the patient, this person could take precedence over someone higher up the list. 'Caring for' is not defined, but in *Re D (Mental Patient: Habeas Corpus)* [2000], the judge said these were 'clear everyday words set in the context where an [AMHP] has to act in a common sense manner … in a situation which is fraught with emotion and difficulty'.

Many patients do not have family or relatives or may have lost touch with them. As the role is intended to provide a safeguard, the Code advocates for an NR to be appointed by application to the county court (s.29 and Code ch. 5).

5-year rule. Finally, and rather oddly, in s.26(7) the Act makes provision for someone other than a relative, with whom the patient has been living for not less than five years, to be the NR (unless the patient is married or someone else in the hierarchical list is also living with or caring for the patient). This was probably added to the list for patients who may have been living in residential care with no relatives, but it can make for some odd situations in practice if the eldest person in a care home is identified as the NR of another resident.

Child arrangements orders and young persons in care

Sections 27 and 28 clarify who the NR may be for children and young persons under care orders or certain child arrangement orders. The AMHP is required to clarify who has PR when assessing a child or young person and whether there are any relevant orders (Code para 19.8).

Delegation. The NR can choose to delegate their functions to someone willing to take on the role, and in this case, the NR should notify the patient (as well as the person whom the relative has authorised to take on the role). Certain rules apply and are detailed in Regulation 24 (England) or Regulation 33 (Wales) (MHA Regulations 2008).

Delegation can last for as long as both parties agree (although it would be advisable for AMHPs to check that the NR would still be regarded as such if the role was delegated some time ago). Any such delegation should be lodged with the relevant detaining authority or local authority. Should the patient be unhappy with this, the only recourse is for the patient to apply to court (see below).

Power to order discharge – section 23. The NR's power to order discharge of their relative from detention or CTO is seen as 'an important extra safeguard' (Hale 2010) in upholding right to liberty. NRs can do so by giving 72 hours' notice to the hospital managers of their intention. The RC can 'block' this order only if he or she certifies that the patient would be 'likely to act in a manner dangerous to other persons or to himself' (s.25(1)). This phrase, commonly mistaken as the initial detention grounds, requires a higher threshold of 'risk' to be established before such discharge could be blocked.

Where discharge of a s.3 or 17A patient is blocked, the NR is prevented from ordering discharge for six months but can apply to the MHT for consideration of the case.

Note s.7 guardianship orders cannot be blocked and therefore would end if the NR made such an order.

Appointment by the county court of acting nearest relative – section 29. S.29 sets out who can apply to the county court for the appointment of an NR and when the court can direct that the functions of the NR be exercised by another person. An AMHP, any relative of the patient, anyone else with whom the patient is residing or the patient could make an application to the court (s.29(2)).

Certain timescales apply to the appointment of an acting NR, depending on what grounds the application is made under. The Reference Guide in Chapter 2 provides a helpful outline of timescales.

Appointing someone to act as a nearest relative. An application to the county court may be made where the patient either has no NR or it is not reasonably practicable to ascertain whether he or she has an NR or who that person is (s.29(3)(a)), or where the NR appears to be incapable of acting due to mental disorder or other illness (s.29(3)(b)).

AMHPs can apply to court when they think it 'necessary or proper' to make an application for s.3 (s.13) and the NR unreasonably objects (s.29(3)(c)). The court will then consider the evidence and decide whether that objection is unreasonable.

The AMHP should also apply if the NR has 'exercised without due regard to the welfare of the patient or the interests of the public, his power to discharge the patient, or is likely to do so' (s.29(3)(d)).

In cases where the patient is detained under s.2 when an application is made under s.29(3)(c) or (d), the court can make an interim order (where urgent) which has the effect of 'freezing' the s.2 while the application is heard.

Unsuitable to act as such. Prior to the 2007 amendments to the Act, the patient was unable to apply to court. This led to much debate during the passage of the bill through Parliament about the possibility of removing the role of NR and replacing it with a chosen person. The case of *JT v UK* [2000] raised the issue of incompatibility where the patient was unable to apply to court to remove her NR.

The patient was subsequently added to the list of people who may apply to the court, and an additional ground was added in s.29(3)(e), that the 'nearest relative of the patient is otherwise not a suitable person to act as such'.

Where there is an NR, this person is a party to the court proceedings and has a right to make representations. There are practical problems for patients and NRs with s.29, and in reality, legal aid is means tested and funding may not be available. Court can be intimidating, and assistance may be necessary to guide someone through the process. Although there is no need for a relative who is the subject of an application above to have legal representation (*CX v LA* [2011]), both the patient and relative should be enabled to understand the process and their part in it. The Code recommends that AMHPs should 'bear in mind that some patients may wish to apply to displace their NR but may be deterred from doing so by the need to apply to the County Court' (para 5.13). Although the decision to apply lies with the AMHP personally, the local authority on whose behalf they are acting is required to have policies in place to assist AMHPs in making this decision (para 5.17). It is questionable whether the additions in the amendments go far enough to uphold patients' A8 rights.

If the applicant cannot provide anyone suitable to take on the role, the court may make the LA the NR. In practice, replacing an inappropriate NR with a named person in the local authority may be of limited use as a safeguard (Gostin 2010), and certainly the named person should be far removed from any team involved with the patient.

On-the-spot questions	In what way is the role of the NR an important safeguard? What could patients do if they were unhappy with their NR, and who might assist them with this?

The Mental Health Tribunal

Mental Health Tribunals provide judicial oversight and review detained patients' cases, and they are perhaps the key safeguard against arbitrary or unfounded detention.

Background, legislative framework, constitution and social work roles

Prior to the 1959 Mental Health Act, detention in hospital required judicial scrutiny *before* the event in that a magistrates' or county court judge needed to 'certify' a person's detention. The 1959 Act established the procedures that remain in the current legislation in that an application for admission to hospital could be made by the NR of the patient or a mental welfare officer (MWO – the distant ancestor of the current AMHP), founded on medical recommendations. As the application to detain was now in the hands of professionals rather than the courts, then, alongside this reform, came the establishment of the Mental Health Review Tribunal (as it was then called) to provide judicial scrutiny after the event (see Eldergill 1997).

It is the Mental Health Tribunal that, in respect of patients detained under the MHA, addresses the requirements of Article 5(4), ECHR:

> Everyone who is deprived of his liberty by arrest or detention shall be entitled to take proceedings by which the lawfulness of his detention shall be decided speedily by a court and his release ordered if the detention is not lawful.

The MHT is a court, although the procedure has been described as 'inquisitorial rather than adversarial' (*W v Egdell* [1989]), but in a fully contested Tribunal hearing one might struggle to see the distinction.

In most cases, the burden of proof is on the detaining authority (i.e. the hospital) to positively satisfy the MHT that the grounds for the detention or CTO continue to be met (*R(H) v MHRT* [2001]) and the standard of proof applied to disputed issues is on the balance of probabilities, which is the standard applied by the courts in civil proceedings (*R(AN) v MHRT* [2005]).

The First-tier Tribunal (Mental Health) is the correct title in England. However, it is much more commonly referred to as the Mental Health Tribunal (MHT). The current organisation of the English Tribunal system (not just in mental health cases) was established by the Tribunals Courts and Enforcement Act 2007. The Act also established the Upper-tier Tribunal, which deals with appeals from both the English and Welsh Tribunals and some judicial review applications that would previously have been dealt with by the High Court.

Section 65, MHA, provides for the establishment of a separate Mental Health Review Tribunal for Wales with its own rules and guidance.

The statutory framework for the operation of the MHT is found within Part V, MHA, 1983. This sets out the statutory rules governing who can apply, when an application can, or when a reference must or can, be made to the MHT, and the legal criteria for each category of patient to which the MHT applies when considering whether detention or compulsion in the community should continue.

The detailed procedural rules for the operation of the MHT are set out in the Tribunal Procedure (First-tier Tribunal) (Health, Education and Social Care Chamber) Rules 2008. The rules deal with matters such as evidence, witnesses and time limits. The right to a fair trial under Article 6 ECHR underlies these judicial rules and is given explicit expression in Rule 2(1): 'The overriding objective of these Rules is to enable the Tribunal to deal with cases fairly and justly.' It is incumbent on all parties in Tribunal proceedings to assist the Tribunal in furthering the overriding objective (Rule 2(4)).

In addition, the Tribunal will, from time to time, issue guidance and Practice Directions dealing with specific matters. The most relevant to social workers is the Practice Direction First-tier Tribunal, Health Education and Social Care Chamber, Statements and Reports in Mental Health Cases (2013), which sets out the requirements for the contents of professionals' reports submitted to the MHT. The key documents that the responsible authority is required to provide to the Tribunal are a medical report, a nursing report and a social circumstances report.

In terms of the social work role, it would be usual for the patient's CC (who could be a social worker) to prepare the social circumstances report for the Tribunal and to give oral evidence at the Tribunal hearing. However, the professional background of the author is not defined by the law or the rules; neither is the author's attendance to provide oral evidence to the Tribunal (*AF v Nottinghamshire* [2015]). The Practice Direction requirements for these reports are detailed, but the report should deal with, among other things, issues such as home and family circumstances; availability of accommodation, community treatment and support, and the patient's previous responses to community follow-up; views of the patient and the NR; and the patient's strengths.

On-the-spot question	What do you think is the value of the social circumstances report to the Tribunal's decision-making?

The issue of whether information in the reports for the Tribunal can be withheld from the patient has been the subject of a number of important Upper-tier Tribunal decisions. Practitioners preparing reports need to exercise caution on this issue. Relatives may commonly want to express views that they would not want the patient to be aware of for fear of damaging their relationship or fear of an angry or aggressive response from the patient, and practitioners themselves may be concerned that their therapeutic relationship with the patient may be harmed by information in the report. However, the withholding or disclosure of information to the patient is a matter for the Tribunal governed by Rule 14 of the Tribunal Rules, and the test is that disclosure would cause a risk of serious harm to the patient or another person as well as it being in the interests of justice and proportionate for the information to be withheld. It is fair to say that the bar for withholding information has now been set extremely high:

KEY CASE ANALYSIS

RM v St Andrew's Healthcare [2010] UKUT 119 (AAC)

In RM v St Andrew's [2010], the hospital sought to withhold the fact that the patient was being covertly medicated. It was feared that discovering this would lead the patient to refuse food and drink and suffer serious deterioration in both his mental health and epilepsy control. The Upper-tier held that the patient could not effectively challenge his detention or have a fair hearing as guaranteed by Article 6 ECHR if he was not aware that he was being covertly medicated. The patient's legal interests were effectively given a higher priority than the immediate medical consequences of the disclosure. The key lesson for practitioners is that it is simply not possible to give assurances to third parties that information will not be disclosed to the patient.

Tribunal panels

The specialist lay member of the MHT is required to have experience in 'administration, knowledge of social services or having other suitable qualifications or experience' (Fennell et al. 2013). It would not be unusual for these panel members to come from a social work background. The other MHT panel members are a Tribunal judge (a lawyer, salaried judge, circuit judge or recorder) and a medical member (an independent consultant psychiatrist). Restricted cases are dealt with by senior judges (salaried judge, circuit judge or recorder).

Patients are entitled to legal representation for MHT proceedings and non-means-tested legal aid is available.

Applications and references

Eligibility for patients subject to civil powers and their NRs to apply to the Tribunal is governed by s.66, MHA.

Patients detained under s.2 can apply any time within the first 14 days of the admission. Patients detained under s.3, under CTOs or guardianship orders, can apply to the MHT in each 'renewal period'. So, a patient detained under s.3, for example, can apply once in the first six months, again if the section is renewed for a further six-month period and again each time the section is renewed for a subsequent 12-month period. A change in the patient's status (e.g. a change from s.2 to s.3) will also trigger a further right to make an application.

NR applications to the Tribunal are mainly limited to the circumstances when a barring order (s.25, MHA) has been issued by the RC in response to an NR's order for discharge of a section 3 or CTO or when the NR has been 'displaced' following a court order appointing an NR under s.29 MHA.

Access to the MHT for patients subject to Part III orders is more limited. The general rule being that, if a court has considered the case at the outset of the order, then the patient may not apply to the Tribunal until the second six months of the detention. There are also a number of shorter-term court orders where there is no right to apply to the MHT at all. For unrestricted hospital order patients, the NR may apply to the MHT whenever the patient would be entitled to apply; however, restricted patients effectively have no NR so there are no Tribunal application rights. The limitations are less for s.37 guardianship order patients who may apply within the first 6 months and during each subsequent renewal period, although not having any power to discharge the NR can also apply to the Tribunal in the first 12 months and in each further 12-month period.

But what of the patient who is unable to access legal advice or representation or unable to effectively make use of their rights to challenge their detention by way of an application to the MHT, perhaps due to the patient being in a particularly acute phase of illness or the patient having a significant learning disability?

S.68, MHA, provides a further safeguard in placing a duty on hospital managers to refer the patient's case to the Tribunal in certain circumstances. For patients subject to civil powers, the hospital must refer the case if six months have elapsed from the date of detention and must refer both civil and unrestricted Part III patients if three years have elapsed since the case was previously considered by the MHT. The MHT has the power to appoint a legal representative for the patient if they lack capacity to appoint themselves (Rule 11). A reference must also be made when a CTO is revoked or when a conditionally discharged patient is recalled to hospital.

In addition, the Secretary of State has discretion to refer an unrestricted patient's case to the Tribunal if he thinks fit (s.67, MHA) even if the patient does not have a statutory entitlement to a Tribunal application. For example, if a patient has missed the 14-day deadline to appeal against detention under s.2 through no fault of their own.

Finally, the Secretary of State must refer the case of a restricted patient to the MHT if 3 years have elapsed since the MHT last considered the case, and also has a general discretion to refer cases (s.71, MHA).

The legal criteria

Broadly speaking the legal criteria that the Tribunal applies mirror the grounds for detention discussed in the previous chapters. For example, when considering the case of a patient detained under s.2, MHA, the legal criteria the Tribunal must apply are found within s.72(1)(a) MHA:

> s.72(1)(a) The Tribunal shall direct the discharge of a patient liable to be detained under section 2 above if [it is] not satisfied
>
> (i) that he is then suffering from a mental disorder or from mental disorder of a nature or degree which warrants his detention in hospital for assessment (or for assessment followed by medical treatment) for at least a limited period; or
> (ii) that his detention as aforesaid is justified in the interests of his own health or safety or with a view to the protection of other persons.

S.72 deals with the legal criteria for all categories of unrestricted and community patients, and s.73 deals with the criteria for restricted patients.

Powers in respect of unrestricted patients (s.72 MHA)

The most important power available to the Tribunal is to discharge a patient from detention (or from a CTO or guardianship order). The wording 'shall direct the discharge … if not satisfied' means that the Tribunal is under a positive duty to discharge if not satisfied as to any of the criteria.

The Tribunal also has a (rarely used) general discretion to discharge even if it is satisfied that the legal criteria are made out.

In addition to the discharge power, the Tribunal has the following further statutory powers:

- Deferred discharge: to discharge from detention at a later date, for example to allow time for necessary community treatment and support to be arranged.

- Statutory recommendations: to facilitate discharge at a later date, the Tribunal may recommend that the patient is transferred to another hospital, for example to a less secure setting; recommend the patient be given leave from hospital under s.17, MHA; recommend that the patient be transferred into guardianship; or recommend that the responsible clinician considers making a CTO. Although the Tribunal cannot compel the hospital to comply with a statutory recommendation, if a recommendation is not followed, it is open to the Tribunal to reconvene to further consider the patient's case.

It is open to the patient to seek any or all of these powers to be exercised.

On-the-spot *question*	Why might the Tribunal make recommendations rather than use its power to discharge?

The Tribunal also has a wide range of 'case management' powers under the Tribunal Procedure Rules and has a wide discretion on matters such as evidence, witnesses, adjournments and timescales to meet the 'over-riding objective' of dealing with cases fairly and justly (Rule 2).

Following the decision in *AH v West London MH NHS Trust* [2011], a patient is entitled to request a public hearing.

For patients in the community under either guardianship or CTOs, the Tribunal's power is limited to discharge, and there is no power to amend conditions or requirements under these orders.

Powers in respect of restricted patients (s.73, s.74, s.75 MHA)

For restricted patients detained in hospital, the Tribunal's powers are limited to granting an absolute or conditional discharge or deferring a direction for conditional discharge (e.g. to allow time for aftercare planning); there are no powers to make statutory recommendations and no discretionary power to discharge. The Tribunal can make what are known as 'extra-statutory recommendations', which, though of no legal force, may be useful in encouraging the hospital to consider matters such as leave or progression to lesser security. This is not a legal power of the Tribunal, and the Upper-tier Tribunal has made it clear that there is no obligation on the Tribunal to consider such applications (*EC v Birmingham* [2012]).

For patients transferred from prison with a restriction direction or for a patient subject to a hybrid order under s.45A with a limitation direction, the Tribunal's powers are further limited, and, in effect, if the Tribunal is of the view that the patient would be eligible for an absolute or conditional discharge if the patient were subject to a restriction order (i.e. s.37/41), the final decision remains with the Secretary of State, and the Tribunal may merely notify the Secretary of State of its opinion.

For conditionally discharged restricted patients, the Tribunal may grant an absolute discharge but may also vary the conditions the patient was discharged under (or impose new conditions).

Procedure

The Tribunal has wide discretion on how the case is managed. However, the usual course of events following an application or reference to the Tribunal would be as follows:

- The detaining authority will be notified of the proceedings and required to file: a summary statement (known as a Part A statement) setting out basic information regarding the patient, the services involved and the patient's detention; and a medical report, nursing report and social circumstances report as discussed above. It would be usual for the hospital's MHA administrator to liaise with the relevant professionals regarding the filing of the reports. The reports are to be filed within three weeks of the hospital having notice of the proceedings, except in s.2 cases, where the proceedings are arranged quickly, and therefore reports must be available at least one hour before the hearing. In restricted cases, the Secretary of State must be notified of the proceedings and may submit a statement of information and comments to the MHT.
- S.2 cases must be heard within seven days of the application (Rule 37). Other cases (s.3, s.37, etc.) do not have a defined timescale, but in practice the hearings would usually be listed within four to eight weeks of the application or reference. For restricted cases, the hearing would usually be listed within 13 weeks.
- If it has been requested (or always in s.2 cases), the medical member of the Tribunal will visit the patient before the hearing to conduct a 'pre-hearing examination' of the patient's condition.
- The Tribunal may permit observers into the hearing if a written request has been made in advance, and we would recommend any practitioner to try to observe at least one Tribunal before attending a hearing to

give evidence; being rigorously questioned and cross-examined in a hearing can sometimes come as a surprise to professionals.

- The formal rules of evidence for court proceedings do not apply in Tribunals, and generally a degree of informality will be applied in order to avoid undue stress on the patient. Equally, Tribunals are legal proceedings, and it can be a valuable message to patients to see that their detention is taken very seriously. Usually, the judge will make introductions and a summary of the procedure for the patient's benefit. The patient's legal representative may be asked to give a brief statement setting out what the patient is seeking from the Tribunal and which of the statutory criteria are in dispute.

- The order of evidence is not defined in any rules, and there may be circumstances where it is helpful to patients to give their evidence at the outset as it may be very difficult for some patients to sit through a large amount of disputed professional evidence without having their say. If the patient has a legal representative, this person will assist the patient to present their evidence by asking questions of the patient. If there has been a pre-hearing examination, a summary of this will be given by the panel.

- Ideally, the authors of the various reports will be in attendance. Each professional will be asked to give oral evidence on any updating matters and may then be questioned both by the Tribunal panel and the legal representative (or the patient if not represented). In most cases, much of the questioning on the statutory criteria will be directed towards the RC.

- Questions of the CC (or representative of the community team) will generally be led by the specialist lay member.

- Once the evidence has been heard, the legal representative will make what are known as submissions – setting out the patient's case, the applications being made to the Tribunal and drawing on any evidence supportive to the patient's case.

- At the conclusion of the hearing, all parties will leave, and the panel will deliberate. Usually, a verbal decision will be given on the day, and written reasons for the Tribunal's decision will be provided at a later date.

The significance of the Tribunal as a safeguard against unnecessary or disproportionate detention or community intervention can be seen in the most recent CQC report on the use of the MHA (2013–14): in this period the statistics reveal that the rate of discharge by the MHT of all categories of detained patient was just under 9 per cent and for patients on CTOs, just over 5 per cent (CQC 2015b). The statistics do not include statutory recommendations that may have assisted patients.

Hospital managers

We have considered hospital managers' duties to refer cases to the Tribunal in certain circumstances. In addition, hospital managers have a number of further safeguarding functions in relation to patients subject to compulsory powers under the MHA.

Under s.23, hospital managers have the power to order the discharge of all categories of unrestricted patients detained in hospital or subject to CTOs (note – for guardianship patients, powers under the order and the power to discharge guardianship orders are held by the local authority rather than the hospital). They have no power to discharge restricted patients or patients remanded to hospital or under interim hospital orders from the courts. The hospital managers have no power to make statutory recommendations, and their powers are limited to discharging or not.

The MHA Code provides that the managers must hold a review following the renewal of a section; should hold a review if the patient requests it or if an NR is 'barred' by the responsible clinician (s.25); and may hold a review at any other time.

The process for review of patients' detention or community treatment is found in ch. 38 of the Code. The review responsibilities are generally delegated to panels of three persons appointed (but not directly employed) by the NHS Trust or private hospital. The procedure for the review of cases described in the Code draws heavily on the practice and procedure of the Tribunal, and to the untrained eye, a hospital manager's hearing might well be indistinguishable from a Tribunal hearing. However, unlike Tribunals, there are no procedural or evidential rules, and the format of reviews can vary a great deal. There are also no statutory criteria that the managers must apply when considering whether to discharge a patient, although the Code, when detailing the questions that ought to be considered, mirrors the statutory criteria applied by the Tribunal (para 38.15–38.18).

We are not aware of any national data regarding the outcomes of hospital managers' reviews, and unlike Tribunal data, this information is not included in the CQC's annual report. However, the authors' own experience and anecdotal evidence from colleagues across a variety of professions suggest that discharge is very rare. Although acting independently, the hospital managers are, in the end, representatives of the detaining authority and therefore 'can never amount to an "independent and impartial Tribunal" within the meaning of Article 6(1) of the ECHR' (Hale 2010). One might therefore wonder to what extent such reviews are truly a safeguard for the patient. However, a review may be of assistance to a patient who perhaps does not have a Tribunal application available; a manager's review can be a useful testing of the water for a patient undecided about whether to submit an application to the Tribunal, and for the patient not contesting detention or CTO, it does at least provide some degree of automatic review on each and every renewal of a detention or CTO, given that there may be an interval of three years between automatic references to the Tribunal.

The hospital managers have a number of further duties and responsibilities defined by both the Code of Practice and the MHA. These will generally be delegated to designated staff at the hospital. The key ones in respect of safeguarding patients' rights are presented here:

- To scrutinise the section papers and ensure the authority to detain is valid (s.15 MHA and Code para 35, para 37.12).
- To provide patients with information about their right to an independent mental health advocate (s.130D and Code para 37.14)
- To provide information to patients and relatives regarding the provisions of the MHA relevant to them and their legal rights (s.132 and s.133 MHA).

To ensure an age-appropriate environment to patients under the age of 18 admitted to hospital (whether under section or informally) (s.131A MHA).

PRACTICE FOCUS

Mr Wood is in hospital on s.2. The RC wishes to make a medical recommendation for s.3 and has called the AMHP. Mr Wood has bipolar disorder, and the RC believes that he remains unwell and in need of a fuller period of treatment in hospital.

- What procedural safeguards exist before the AMHP can apply for s.3?
- If Mr Wood is made subject to s.3, what treatment could he be given without his consent?
- When could Mr Wood apply to the MHT, and what powers does it have?
- If Mrs Wood, as nearest relative, is unhappy with any of the above at any stage, what could she do?

The Care Quality Commission (CQC) (England) and the Health Inspectorate (Wales)

The CQC and Health Inspectorate Wales are regulatory authorities within the Health & Social Care Act 2008. They have registration, review and investigation functions as well as specific functions under the MHA.

Previous mental health law has required an independent body to oversee and protect the rights of patients when their liberty is curtailed, the original body being the Lunacy Commission. The Mental Health Act Commission (MHAC) was established with the 1983 Act and later sub-sumed into the Care Quality Commission (CQC) in 2008 via the Health & Social Care Act.

The CQC has powers to inspect and regulate health and social services. It does so by inspecting against standards of care and promoting good practice. It continues to have special functions in relation to the MHA. This allows the CQC to use its overall powers (such as enforcement powers in the Health & Social Care Act 2008) to require providers to meet the necessary standards.

Under the MHA, the CQC has a duty to 'keep under review and where appropriate, investigate the exercise of the powers and discharge of the duties conferred by the Act in relation to the detention of patients, reception of patients in guardianship or patients who are liable to be detained under the Act, CTO patients or those on guardianship' (s.120).

The CQC has the following powers and responsibilities:

- To make arrangements for CQC inspectors/reviewers to visit and inter-view patients in private (whether they are detained in hospital, subject to CTO or guardianship), and in doing so, to have the right of access to patients and their relevant records
- To interview doctors or ACs in private
- To investigate any complaints by patients in certain circumstances
- To publish reports as a result of any inspection and can direct the hospi-tal manager or local authority to publish an action statement as a result
- To publish an annual report on the use of the MHA and DoLS
- To appoint SOADs
- To make proposals to the Secretary of State on the content of the English Code of Practice (s.118)
- To review the deaths of certain patients while in the custody of the State
- To review the withholding of mail (s.134)

Other legal safeguards

Finally, the law beyond the MHA provides two further potential remedies to patients seeking to challenge their detention:

Habeas corpus. A detained person (under MHA powers or otherwise) may apply to the High Court for a writ of habeas corpus (Latin for 'you have the body'). It is an ancient legal principle safeguarding against arbitrary detention and provides that those responsible for the detention must justify the lawfulness of the detention – a failure to provide the justification will lead to the person's release.

Such an application would be appropriate in mental health cases where there has been a procedural error that renders the detention unlawful on the face of the presenting facts, for example, a fundamental defect in the section papers. The most widely cited case example is *Re: S-C* [1996], where the approved social worker (who would now be the AMHP), knowing that the NR of the patient objected to an application for detention under s.3 MHA being made, consulted another relative and entered that person's details on the s.3 application. The detention was therefore demonstrably unlawful from the outset.

Judicial review. A detained patient may also apply to the High Court (or now the Upper-tier Tribunal) for judicial review of the decision to detain. The distinction between habeas corpus and judicial review is a subtle one, but essentially, an application for judicial review will seek to show a flaw in the decision-making process that led to the detention, even where, on the face of it, the detention is lawful. The grounds for judicial review applications are limited and defined; the most relevant grounds for an application in respect of detention under the MHA are:

- Illegality, for example where the decision-maker has taken account of irrelevant matters or failed to take into account relevant matters or failed to understand the relevant legal provisions
- Irrationality, where the decision was one that no reasonable authority could have reached
- Abuse of power, where the decision-maker has failed to follow proper procedure or failed to follow the rules of natural justice
- Human Rights Act 1998, where the decision has breached a person's ECHR rights

Further reading

Administrative Justice and Tribunals Council and Care Quality Commission (2011) *Patients' Experiences of the First-tier Tribunal (Mental Health).* A report focusing on the subjective experience of the patient in Tribunal proceedings.

Fennell, P. W. H., P. Letts and J. Wilson (2013) *Mental Health Tribunals, Law, Policy and Practice.* Detailed text on the law and practice in Tribunal proceedings.

Hewitt, D. (2008) *The Nearest Relative Handbook.* A useful book setting out everything related to nearest relatives.

8

INTERFACE BETWEEN THE MENTAL HEALTH ACT AND THE MENTAL CAPACITY ACT

AT A GLANCE THIS CHAPTER COVERS:

- the Mental Capacity Act
- additional MCA provisions of relevance
- deprivation of liberty and the deprivation of liberty safeguards (DoLS)
- MHA or MCA?
- children, young people, the MHA and consent
- compulsion in the community under the MHA and deprivation of liberty

The Mental Capacity Act

The Mental Capacity Act 2005 (MCA) is intended to be 'enabling and supportive' (MCA Code of Practice ch. 2). Its main aim is to assist those over age 16 to make decisions for themselves, only intervening in their best interests (s.4), if they are unable to make that decision when it needs to be made, as a result of incapacity (s.3).

Empowerment and personal autonomy are key considerations in the MCA. The Act is also intended to discourage carers from being 'overly restrictive or controlling' (MCA Code 1.4). Those working in health and social services should be well acquainted with the MCA and its Code of Practice (e.g. see the Introduction to the MHA Code; and DH 2015b).

Although it is now ten years old, 'prevailing cultures of risk averse and paternalistic practices of social services and health professionals' have been criticised for preventing the Act from becoming widely known or embedded into practice (House of Lords Select Committee 2014). The DH (2014d) has indicated that professionals' responsibility to familiarise themselves with this piece of legislation is a 'basic professional duty'. This applies to anyone working with adults, including a requirement to ensure that an assessment is made of the parents' capacity to give consent to arrangements for their child (*Re CA (A baby): Coventry City Council v C* [2012] and *Newcastle City Council v WM* [2015]).

Although the MHA and MCA are different laws with different purposes and procedures, there are overlaps. The MCA could apply for a wide range of decision-making, much broader than assessment or treatment of mental disorder. The MCA may be just as applicable to someone with mental disorder for decisions about finance, housing, care, relationships and treatment, if they are assessed as lacking capacity to make such decisions.

Section 1 – principles

Section 1 of the MCA sets out the five statutory principles, which must always be applied. These principles include assuming the person has capacity unless it is established otherwise. Those using the MCA must not treat anyone as unable to make a decision unless 'all practicable steps' to help the person make the decision have been taken without success. People can make unwise decisions without this necessarily meaning they lack capacity. Where a lack of capacity is established, decisions made on the person's behalf must be in their best interests, and finally, before anything is done or the decision made, assessors should have regard to options that are less restrictive of the person's rights and freedom of action.

Section 2 – persons who lack capacity

> A person lacks capacity in relation to a matter if at the material time he is unable to make a decision for himself in relation to the matter because of an impairment of, or a disturbance in the functioning of the mind or brain.

Firstly, those assessing capacity need to be clear about what the specific decision is. If any doubt arises as to the person's ability to make that decision, those assessing capacity are required to establish whether difficulty in making the decision is connected with an impairment of or disturbance in the functioning of the mind or brain (*PC v NC & City of York Council* [2013]). Should someone be assessed as having capacity to make a decision, but the ability to do so is impaired by coercion or undue influence, the MCA would not be applicable, but the inherent jurisdiction of the court may be available (*A Local Authority v DL* [2010]).

This impairment or disturbance in the mind or brain could be temporary, for example due to urinary tract infections, the influence of drugs or alcohol, or unconsciousness. It could be fluctuating perhaps as a result of a mental illness, or it could be a more permanent state such as learning disability or brain injury. It should be emphasised, however, that the principles in s.1, MCA, preclude presumptions of incapacity based solely on age, appearance, or simply as a result of a condition such as mental disorder.

Section 3 – the test for assessing capacity

S.3, MCA, sets out the test for assessing capacity and states that a person is unable to make a decision for himself if he is unable to

- understand the information relevant to the decision;
- retain that information;
- use or weigh that information as part of the process of making the decision; or
- communicate his decision (whether by talking, using sign language or any other means).

Information must be given in a way that is appropriate to his circumstances (s.3(2)), and retaining information only for a short period of time does not prevent someone from being regarded as able to make that decision (s.3(3)). The information relevant to making the decision includes the reasonably foreseeable consequences of deciding either way or of failing to make a decision (s.3(4)).

Some decisions are more complicated than others. Inability to make a decision about one thing need not mean someone is unable to make a decision about another; hence the emphasis being on specific decision-making. The decision-maker has to decide, based on the 'balance of probabilities', whether the person lacks capacity. Professionals should never express an opinion without carrying out a proper examination and assessment of the person's capacity to make the decision (MCA Code ch. 4). It is not appropriate or lawful to base an assessment of capacity on the views of family members alone or to make assumptions without directly seeing the person, and could lead to disciplinary proceedings (Community Care 2015).

Having followed sections 1–3, if the person is unable to meet one of the four parts of the capacity test, that person is deemed to lack capacity for the decision in question.

Inability to 'use or weigh' the information relevant to the decision has led to some interesting cases in relation to persons with mental disorder. It also shows a clear overlap between those with mental disorders and the use of the MCA. For examples, see *SB (A patient; Capacity to Consent To Termination)* [2013] and *A County Council v MS and RS* [2014].

The Act has a power to intervene only after it has been proved that the person concerned lacks capacity. More should not be expected of a person when capacity is in doubt than would be expected of someone where capacity is undoubted (*Heart of England NHS Foundation Trust v JB* [2014]).

Section 4 – best interests

Once incapacity has been established for the particular decision, s.4 sets out a statutory best-interests checklist. Such considerations must take account of 'all relevant circumstances' (s.4(2)), including whether the person might regain capacity, the person's past and present wishes and feelings, beliefs and values, and the views of other relevant people (s.4(6)). Finally, the decision-maker must not be motivated by a desire to bring about death (s.4(5)). The Code specifies that best-interest decisions should be recorded, and this should include how the decision was reached and the factors considered in reaching that decision (MCA Code). The court may also have to consider best interests, and in *Wye*

> ## PRACTICE FOCUS
>
> Mike is a 48-year-old divorcee, who has just started a relationship with Mary, a 43-year-old woman. Mike has bipolar disorder and is under the Care Programme Approach (CPA).
>
> Mike has told his community mental health nurse that he intends to book a cruise for himself and Mary. This will cost him all of his savings and leave him with limited funds to return to or pay bills with.
>
> His community mental health nurse has reminded him that he has been in debt before and found this extremely stressful.
>
> Mike tells her that he has always dreamt of having a cruise and falling in love, and it is not evidence that he is becoming manic or not thinking straight.
>
> The nurse is concerned about Mike's current mental state and ability to make this decision. He appears slightly more elated than usual, and she is concerned that he may have stopped his medication.
>
> *How would the principles in s.1 apply, and what should the community mental health nurse consider in ss.2–4 if she remains concerned about Mike's decision-making?*

Valley NHS Trust v Mr B [2015], the judge concluded (taking into account the views and wishes of the person) that it would not be in the best interests of a man with mental illness, assessed as lacking capacity for the decision, to have his leg amputated to save his life.

Additional MCA provisions of relevance

Lasting powers of attorney

Section 9 of the MCA creates lasting powers of attorney (LPAs), and sections 10–14 provide details of the role and its responsibilities and restrictions (including that donees must act in accordance with the principles in section 1 of the MCA). A donor has to be over the age of 18 and confers on the donee the authority to make decisions about all or any personal welfare and/or property and affairs matters. For personal welfare decisions, the LPA will not come into effect unless the donor loses capacity. However, for property and affairs, the LPA can come into effect while the donor has capacity, if the donor wishes. Once an LPA is registered with the Office of the Public Guardian, it will come into effect, as detailed above.

LPAs are substituted decision-makers and therefore must be consulted for any relevant decisions. Best interests still apply. A personal welfare LPA may include decisions around treatment and the power to refuse to consent to treatment for mental disorder.

The donee must have capacity to make the LPA. LPA forms can be downloaded from www.lastingpowerofattorney.service.gov.uk/home.

Section 15 refers to general powers of the court and appointment of deputies.

Court-appointed deputy.

Where the person lacks capacity for personal welfare or property and affairs matters the court's starting point is that they should make any decision themselves. However, they may appoint a deputy or deputies who will act (s.16). The court may appoint a deputy if complicated medical needs and treatments are required, or family members are in dispute over best interests, or there is a conflict between services and family or friends which cannot be resolved. See the MCA Code of Practice at ch. 8 for more details.

Advance decisions to refuse treatment (s.24).

The MCA allows over 18s to make advance decisions refusing treatment. However, Part IV of the MHA can over-rule such advance decisions or decisions of a valid LPA or deputy where the advance decision is a refusal of treatment for mental disorder. Note that in *Nottinghamshire Healthcare NHS Trust and RC* [2014], the court ruled that it would be lawful for the treating hospital not to impose treatment, even though Part IV, MHA, would allow them to and that it would be 'an abuse of power' in that particular instance.

Section 5 – acts in connection with care and treatment

Section 5 provides protection for any acts done in connection with a person's care and treatment. If the person can evidence that he has followed s.1–s.4 of the MCA, he will be protected from liability when undertaking a range of tasks, from basic day-to-day tasks to 'life-changing events' such as decisions about moving home or having medical treatment (MCA Code 6.1). The Code gives a list of possible actions that might be covered by section 5 as well as guidance on what happens in emergency situations (MCA Code ch. 6). In addition, some cases require an independent mental capacity advocate (IMCA) for certain decisions, and some decisions may require further consideration by the Court of Protection.

On-the-spot question	When might s.5 of the Mental Capacity Act be relevant for someone with a mental disorder?

Section 6 – limitations

Section 6 sets out the limitations to section 5. The MCA refers to 'D' as the decision-maker and 'P' as the person who is assessed as lacking capacity for the decision.

Protection in s.5 extends to the use of restraint provided it is proportionate (no more than necessary) to the likelihood of P suffering harm and the seriousness of that harm. Harm could, for example, be financial, physical or psychological. Restraint includes the 'use or threat to use force, to secure the doing of an act which P resists or restricting P's liberty of movement, whether or not P resists' (s.6(4)). This could include physically stopping someone from running into a busy road, if the person has no awareness or understanding of the dangers of traffic. It may involve gently persuading someone to move away from the door if there is a risk of the person leaving to go onto the road.

Any restrictions should be the least intrusive type and minimum amount used for the shortest duration possible. They should be used only to achieve a specific outcome in the best interests of the person lacking capacity. This means that where restraint is only required to prevent or limit risk to others, the provisions of the MCA are not adequate. In these circumstances, either the criteria in the MHA may apply or restraint under common law may, in limited circumstances, be necessary. Note, however, that most of common law has now been integrated into the MCA, and it cannot be relied upon in instances where the MCA should have been used.

In *ZH v Commissioner of Police for the Metropolis* [2012], police failed to adequately assess the situation or apply sections 5 and 6, MCA, in particular, when removing a young man with autism from a swimming pool, where he had become fixated on the water. The restraint they used was disproportionate and amounted to assault and battery, violating Articles 3, 5 and 8.

Although restraint (or restrictions on liberty) is possible within s.5 and s.6, s.4B states that nothing in the MCA authorises such a deprivation except if authorised by a court, or by using Schedule A1, DoLS.

Deprivation of liberty within the MCA has the same meaning as Article 5(1) ECHR, which does not define a deprivation, but rather reminds us that:

> Everyone has the right to liberty and security of person. No-one shall be deprived of his liberty save in the following cases and in accordance with a procedure prescribed by law.
>
> (e) ... persons of unsound mind ...

However, 'it is identifying precisely where the measures lie on the continuum (between restrictions and deprivation) that can sometimes prove so difficult' (Law Society 2015).

Deprivation of liberty and the deprivation of liberty safeguards (DoLS)

Liberty has been a basic human right for some time. In *London Borough of Hillingdon v Neary* [2011], the judge refers again to the Magna Carta.

The Universal Declaration of Human Rights states that 'all human beings are born free and equal in dignity and rights' and that 'everyone has the right to life, liberty and security of person' (A3 UDHR 1948). Article 5 of the European Convention on Human Rights (1950) 'prevents arbitrary or unjustified deprivations of liberty' (*McKay v UK* [2007]).

The State has a positive obligation to uphold the rights of its citizens. It can only interfere with this right if it follows a lawful procedure (such as detention under the MHA for example). Such a procedure should allow the person to take proceedings by which 'the lawfulness of their detention can be decided speedily by a court and their release ordered if the detention is not lawful' (A5(4)). As we shall see later, the State may deprive someone of liberty in a care home or general hospital (or even in their own home), often to enable the person to live safely. In such situations, the MHA would not be relevant, but deprivation of liberty must be authorised if the State is involved.

Establishing a deprivation of liberty within the meaning of A5 ECHR

There are three elements to a deprivation of liberty within the meaning of A5 ECHR, which must all be met:

- The objective element – which means that the person is confined to a certain restricted space for a 'not negligible length of time'.

- The subjective element – the person has not consented to the confinement (or cannot because of a lack of capacity).
- That the State is responsible for the confinement.

The objective element This element has been the subject of much debate about what a 'not negligible length of time' might be and what 'confined' might amount to. Professionals' ability to identify a deprivation was seen to be unreliable, subject to professional bias and inconsistent in application (Cairns et al. 2011). For example, was liberty the same for everyone or was it more appropriate to compare 'like with like'? If someone had multiple physical and learning disabilities, was it reasonable to compare their liberty and lifestyle with someone without such disabilities or was it more realistic to compare then with someone else with similar disabilities and lifestyle (*Cheshire West & Chester CC v P* [2011])? The decision of the Supreme Court in *Cheshire West & Chester Council v P; P & Q v Surrey County Council* [2014] UKSC 19 established that the 'acid test' is whether the person is 'under continuous (or complete) supervision and control and not free to leave' (see Key Case Analysis).

The Supreme Court did not define exactly what continuous supervision and control might mean. However, the case of *Guzzardi v Italy* (1980) is often referred to when identifying what this might mean:

> The starting point must be the specific situation of the individual concerned and account must be taken of a whole range of factors arising in a particular case such as type, duration, effects and manner of implementation of the measure in question. The distinction between a deprivation of and restriction upon liberty is merely one of degree or intensity and not one of nature or substance.

Being free to leave means being free to discharge oneself to live elsewhere, and the Article 8 ECHR right to respect for privacy and family life is highly relevant in such decisions.

The subjective element. Is the person able to consent to the regime or do they lack capacity to do so? Where the person lacks capacity to consent, the subjective element is met.

HL v UK **(2004).** In *HL v UK* (2004), the European Court of Human Rights concluded that HL, a 48-year-old man with autism and learning disability, had been deprived of his liberty unlawfully. He had been discharged to adult foster carers, having lived most of his adult life in

Bournewood Hospital. He lived successfully with his carers for several years, but following an incident at his local day centre (which included self-harm), he was admitted once again to Bournewood as an 'informal' patient under s.131 MHA. He was unable to consent because he lacked capacity to do so.

At the time (1997), informal admissions under the common law were routine procedure for people who lacked capacity to consent but were neither objecting or resisting to the admission or care. This is now commonly termed the 'compliant incapacitated patient'.

Staff believed they were acting in HL's best interests. However, his foster carers challenged Bournewood Hospital by applying to the court for judicial review and a writ of habeas corpus.

The case ended at the European Court of Human Rights, which ruled that his care and treatment had amounted to a deprivation of his liberty, and as it had not been authorised by a procedure prescribed by law, it had been a breach of A5(1), A5(4) and A8. Regardless of HL's compliance, the regime at the hospital was deemed to amount to a deprivation of HL's liberty, requiring lawful authorisation. In deciding that HL's admission amounted to a deprivation of liberty, the court considered the following restrictions:

- HL was conveyed to hospital by ambulance with two nursing staff.
- Sedative medication was given prior to and during the admission.
- His foster carers request for discharge was denied.
- He was unable to leave the hospital.
- He was given treatment and was under continuous supervision of nursing staff. Professionals 'exercised complete and effective control'.
- HL was 'not free to leave'.

The State is responsible. A deprivation of liberty within the meaning of A5 ECHR requires State involvement. For HL, Bournewood Hospital was State involvement, hence the ruling. This significantly changed practice because it effectively ruled that where incapacitated patients were being deprived of their liberty (and could not consent), the State would require legal authorisation to prevent a breach of A5 ECHR. Without this, they are acting unlawfully and contrary to s.6 HRA 1998. Those who are deprived of their liberty unlawfully have a legal right to compensation.

On-the-spot question	Why is it important to have legal authorisation to deprive someone of their liberty?

> **KEY CASE ANALYSIS**

Cheshire West and Chester Council v P; P & Q v Surrey County Council [2014] UKSC 19

P had cerebral palsy and Down's Syndrome, requiring 24-hour care to meet his personal care needs. He moved into accommodation arranged by the local authority in his best interests, following orders from the Court of Protection.

He shared this house with two other residents. P received 98 hours of additional one-to-one support each week to help him leave the house whenever he chose. He went to a day centre four days a week and a hydrotherapy pool on the fifth day. He also went out to a club, the pub and shops and saw his mother regularly at her home and at the day centre.

P required a wheelchair to walk more than short distances and needed prompting with all daily living activities. He wore continence pads, but because he pulled at these and put pieces in his mouth, he wore a 'body suit' to prevent him from getting to the pads and choking. Intervention was also needed to cope with other behaviours that were challenging, but he was not on any tranquillising medication.

P and Q (also known as Mig and Meg) were sisters, living respectively in a foster home and a residential home. Mig lived with a foster mother who would restrain her, in her best interests, if she tried to leave (although she had never tried). Mig had a learning disability, communicated with difficulty and had limited understanding. She spent much time listening to music on her iPod in her bedroom. She needed help to cross the road and was unaware of the danger of traffic. She attended a further education unit daily and was taken on trips and holidays with her foster mother.

Meg lived in a specialised care home for adults with complex needs and occasionally had to be restrained because of her challenging behaviour. She also required medication and continuous supervision and control by staff. Meg attended the same unit as Mig and had 'a much fuller social life than her sister'.

The Supreme Court considered the question of whether or not all three people were deprived of their liberty, or whether, as had been suggested by the Court of Appeal, they were living as normal a life as they could be, given their disabilities. The Supreme Court ruled that the key question is this:

Is the person concerned under continuous supervision and control and not free to leave?

This question was to be asked, regardless of the good intentions of those caring for P and Mig and Meg.

Lady Hale stated that human rights are universal and apply to all. In the ruling she goes on to state the following:

> What it means to be deprived of liberty must be the same for everyone, whether or not they have physical or mental disabilities.
>
> (para 46)

> The fact that my living arrangements are comfortable, and indeed make my life as enjoyable as it could possibly be, should make no difference. A gilded cage is still a cage.
>
> (para 46)

> The local authorities have no doubt done the best they can to make their lives as happy and fulfilled as they possibly could be … but … in the end it is the constraints that matter.
>
> (para 56)

They key issue was not whether the person was objecting or compliant, but the interventions from staff. For people like P, Mig and Meg, decision-makers should 'err on the side of caution' in deciding what constitutes a deprivation of liberty, for adults who were extremely vulnerable. The safeguards should be there to provide additional protection from arbitrary acts and provide the necessary external oversight of the care and treatment provided.

The deprivation of liberty safeguards (DoLS). As a result of the HL case (and others), Parliament identified a gap in the law, commonly termed the 'Bournewood gap'. Where people lacked capacity to consent to their care or treatment in the relevant hospital or care home but were compliant with this care, use of the MHA was not necessarily appropriate or lawful, (e.g. for incapacitated adults in a general hospital for physical health treatment, or in a care home to keep them safe). If people in these situations were deprived of their liberty in their best interests, then Parliament had to develop a 'procedure prescribed by law'.

The DoLS were introduced in 2007. The DoLS Code of Practice, which is supplementary to the MCA Code, explains that the safeguards are a 'legal framework … to prevent breaches of the ECHR such as ones identified in *HL v UK* (DoLS Code introduction). They apply to anyone over 18 years with a mental disorder within the meaning of s.1, MHA, living in a care home or a hospital and lacking capacity to consent to care or treatment there that amounts to a deprivation of liberty. For those with a learning disability, the exclusions in s.1 of the MHA do not apply under DoLS.

DoLS process. This process, set out in Schedule A1 of the MCA, requires certain professionals to assess whether or not specific grounds are met before a deprivation of liberty can be authorised.

Authorisations to deprive a person of his liberty are made by the supervisory body (SB), which is the relevant local authority. The care home or hospital where the person is or will be residing is termed the managing authority (MA).

The MA must refer a person to the SB for a DoLS assessment if he or she believes that someone is or will be deprived of liberty in the care home or hospital. An urgent authorisation can be made but must be followed up by assessment for a standard authorisation, which can last up to one year.

The qualifying requirements necessitate six assessments, undertaken by a best interests assessor (BIA) and a mental health assessor. The qualifying requirements are set out in Part 3 of Schedule A1 and include:

Table 8.1: Schedule A1, Mental Capacity Act 2005 – Summary

Age – P must be 18 years old or over.
No Refusals – whether any authorisation would conflict with an existing decision relating to the person, for example an advance decision to refuse treatment or a decision of an LPA or a court-appointed deputy.
Mental Capacity – The person must lack capacity to decide whether to be accommodated in the care home or hospital for the relevant care or treatment.
Mental Health – The person must be suffering from a mental disorder within the meaning of s.1, MHA, with no exclusions for those with learning disabilities. DoLS Code guidance indicates that this assessment must also take into consideration how the deprivation of liberty is likely to affect the person; for example will it exacerbate his or her mental state, or will it make no difference to the person?
Eligibility – whether the person is ineligible to be on a DoLS authorisation; see below. The double negative in the schedule (referring to P as 'not ineligible') has been the subject of much criticism for being difficult to understand.
Best Interests – The BIA must assess whether a deprivation of liberty has occurred or is likely to occur and, if so, whether it is in the best interests of the person with reference to s.4–s.6.

Eligibility assessment. The eligibility assessment checks whether the person is eligible to be placed under DoLS. In plain language, there would be no need to be detained or compelled for the same purpose more than once.

In summary, the person will be 'ineligible' to be detained under DoLS if

- already detained as a hospital in-patient under the MHA or liable to be detained; or
- on s.17 leave, a CTO (s.17A) or guardianship (s.7 or s.37) or Conditional Discharge (s.37/41), and a DoLS authorisation would be 'inconsistent with an obligation placed on them under the MHA, such as a requirement to live somewhere else' (DoLS Code para 4.41); or
- is 'within the scope' of the MHA, meaning an application for s.2 or s.3 could be made.

Where DoLS applies, conditions may be attached to the authorisation. Safeguards include the appointment of an independent mental capacity advocate (IMCA), a relevant persons representative (RPR), reviews by the MA at certain points and at any point when requested by the RPR and access to the Court of Protection. The SB should keep the regime under review and continue to consider less restrictive interventions that might not necessitate detention.

The DoLS have been the subject of much debate and criticism, including the difficulty in identifying exactly what a deprivation looked like (particularly prior to the Cheshire West Supreme Court ruling). They were used much less than had been expected in their first year (House of Lords 2014, para 262), and it was considered that many incapacitated adults were not able to access the safeguards intended by the DoLS regime.

In *LB Hillingdon v Neary* [2011], the local authority deprived Steven Neary of his liberty by insisting that he reside at a care home and not be allowed to return home to his father. In doing so, they acted unlawfully by depriving him of his liberty at the care home and paying insufficient regard to A8 ECHR. In fact, the court considered that the DoLS could not be used by the SB to stifle an objection by family or carers. Such cases require referral to the Court of Protection.

Since the Supreme Court ruling in *Cheshire West*, referrals to the SB have increased significantly (DH 2015) because the threshold for what constitutes a deprivation of liberty has been lowered. Furthermore, as the DoLS do not meet the needs of those living in supported living arrangements or in their own homes, a new gap has been identified. In these instances, the Court of Protection is required to consider authorising the deprivation of liberty. The important issue of children and young people and deprivation of liberty has been raised in several cases and emphasises the significance of this ruling for education and children's services (see *re AB (A child: deprivation of liberty)* [2015] EWHC 3125 (Fam); *Re D (a child: deprivation of liberty)* [2015] EWHC 922 (Fam)).

Critics of the DoLS suggested that identifying a 'deprivation of liberty' was overly complex, and the safeguards 'not fit for purpose' (House of Lords 2014). The terminology was considered to put managing authorities off from making the necessary applications. 'Depriving' someone of anything was potentially seen to be a negative intervention rather than a positive obligation in the best interests of the person. Hospitals and care homes misunderstood, on many occasions, exactly what might constitute a deprivation of liberty, and if so, what to do next.

The Law Commission launched a three-year review of DoLS in 2014, but due to pressure, the timescale for the final report, which was due in summer 2017, was moved forward to summer 2016. This will include proposals for a new statute to meet the requirements of the Supreme Court ruling in *Cheshire West*.

At the time of writing, the Government has responded to the Law Commission's initial proposals, including concern that 'the proposed system is unnecessarily complex'. One imagines it could not become any more complex than its predecessor (DH 2015).

MHA or MCA?

Given all of the above, professionals have understandably struggled to make sense of when to use the MCA or MHA when considering an admission to a psychiatric hospital for assessment or treatment of a mental disorder. Conclusions in the MCA scrutiny report called for urgent assistance for practitioners trying to clarify the interface between the MCA and MHA.

MHA Code principles dictate that the 'least restrictive' option should be considered, and chapter 13.11 of the MCA Code states that 'if a clinician believes that they can safely assess or treat a person under the MCA, they do not need to consider using the MHA. In this situation it would be difficult to meet the requirements of the MHA anyway'.

Informal admissions are insufficient where a deprivation of liberty is likely to take place and the patient cannot or does not consent. Further legal authorisation is required for such admissions, and the choices are either the DoLS, MHA or in some circumstances an order from the Court of Protection.

In relation to admission for assessment or treatment of mental disorder, decision-makers must rule out all other community options first before looking at admissions and detention. They must also ensure that in discussions about potential admission for assessment or treatment, people are enabled to make the decision themselves where possible, whether to consent to an admission or not. This entails providing someone with adequate information. The information they require will be case specific, but s.1(3) suggests that practicable steps must be taken to help someone decide whether to consent. If they cannot consent due to a lack of capacity, this must be recorded along with the information they were offered (see MHA Code of Practice para 13.22). *A PCT v LDV* [2013] and *Re NRA & Others* [2015] indicate the information that may be relevant to the decision. In para 211 of *NRA & Ors*, the judge states that 'consent must be based on a properly informed and fair decision-making process', and in *Stankov v Bulgaria* the European Court emphasises that consent must be established during

> the course of a fair and appropriate procedure, and that all necessary information concerning the placement and the proposed treatment was provided to the person concerned in an adequate fashion.

More recently, in *Secretary of State for Justice v KC and C Partnership NHS Foundation Trust* [2015] UKUT 376, the court held that

> the right to give or refuse consent to something is an expression of the autonomy of the individual and thus the state has a duty to respect that expression of autonomy under article 8 ECHR. That right applies equally to a detained mental health patient who has capacity as it applies to any other person.

> (para 133)

In *AM v South London & Maudsley NHS Foundation Trust* [2013], categories of patient were defined as follows at para 17, specifically in relation to remaining in hospital for assessment or treatment for a mental disorder (but also helpful in a broader context):

The following should then be considered:

Table 8.2: Consent and Capacity – Categories of Patient

Patients who are capacitated and consent	s.131, MHA, informal admission, although decision-makers can consider use of MHA if consent is not reliable or risks suggest a change of mind. See chapter 14.14–14.17 of the MHA Code of Practice.
Patients who are capacitated and refuse or object	The MHA would be required. For more detail on what might constitute an objection, see MHA Code para 13.51, DoLS Code para 4.46–47 and Schedule 1A.
Patients who lack capacity but object or resist (or previous information suggests they would if they are unable to communicate this) or who have a valid LPA or donee who objects on their behalf	The MHA would be required.
Patients who lack capacity but are compliant (meaning there is no objection or likelihood of an objection)	The relevant questions are whether the MCA would be adequate or whether there is a likelihood that the person may be deprived of their liberty. If so, further legal authorisation is necessary. This could be authorisation under DoLS, the MHA or an order from the Court of Protection. See MHA Code para 13.49.

In making decisions about how to authorise a deprivation of liberty, decision-makers are advised by the MHA Code not to assume one regime has more safeguards or is less restrictive than the other (MHA Code ch. 13), but to consider what might be most appropriate in the individual case.

Children, young people, the MHA and consent

The MHA can apply to children and young people under 18 years, although the application of the Act would be for a very small group of children where alternatives have been ruled out. The MHA Code of Practice differentiates between young people who are aged 16–17 years and children who are under 16 years. This mirrors the categories in the MCA and is used in the discussion below in relation to children, young people and consent.

The following elements are important considerations when assessing for hospital admission for assessment or treatment of mental disorder.

- The age of the child (under 16 years) or young person (16–17 years)
- The child's competence or a young person's capacity to consent
- Parental responsibility (PR) and parental consent
- Confidentiality and the wishes of the child or young person
- Decisions about admission to hospital and treatment in hospital are, of course, linked but should be assessed separately
- Use of MHA, MCA or Children Act or in some cases authorisation of the courts
- Deprivation of liberty
- Involvement of professionals with particular expertise and experience with children and young people with mental disorder

In all instances, a child or young person should be given adequate information and assisted in the decision-making process. The MHA Code gives guidance in chapter 19.

Children and young people may find decisions about admission and treatment of a mental disorder overwhelming and unusual. This may affect their ability to decide and should be borne in mind by professionals.

Those with PR may be able to consent on behalf of a young person who lacks capacity or a child who is not Gillick competent (see later explanation of Gillick competence). Decision-makers need to consider each individual case and whether those with PR can reasonably be expected to make the decision in question. The Code refers to the 'scope of parental responsibility' when considering what types of decisions might be made by a person with PR and the limitations on this. In all cases, those with PR 'have a central role in relation to decisions about admission and treatment of their child' (para 19.6).

Young people aged 16–17 years

Those with PR should be involved in decisions about best interests if the young person lacks capacity to consent to admission or treatment. In these circumstances, those with PR may consent on behalf of an incapacitated young person. However, decision-makers must consider whether this is a decision that those with PR can make. See below for consideration of deprivation of liberty.

Where young persons aged 16–17 are assessed as having capacity to make decisions about admission or treatment, and they consent, this is adequate, and informal admission is likely to be sufficient (s.131(4)). Where a capacitated young person does not consent, it would be necessary to use either the MHA or to seek the authorisation of the court. In neither case would it be appropriate to rely on parental consent. The same applies where a young person is not incapacitated but cannot decide because of the enormity or overwhelming nature of the decision and further legal authorisation should be sought.

Children under 16 years

For those under 16 years, the relevant assessment of Gillick competence (*Gillick v West Norfolk and Wisbech Area Health Authority* [1986]) is similar to that of the MCA (see ch. 19.34–19.37 of MHA Code for details). As the code states, 'the concept of Gillick competence reflects the child's increasing development to maturity' (19.35).

Where children are assessed as Gillick competent for decisions about admission and treatment of a mental disorder, they can consent or refuse, and in neither case is it adequate to rely on parental consent. However, those with PR should be involved in the decision-making process and assist the child as much as possible where appropriate. Equally, if the child is Gillick competent but overwhelmed by the nature of the decision, it is not adequate to rely on parental consent. Further legal authority would be necessary, either via the MHA or, if not applicable, the courts.

For children assessed as lacking Gillick competence, it is possible to rely on parental consent but issues of deprivation of liberty should form part of the considerations.

Deprivation of liberty and under 18s

A5(1) and deprivation of liberty has no lower age limit. Where children lack competence or young people lack capacity to consent to admission or treatment for mental disorder, it is necessary to consider the restrictions placed upon them and whether these amount to a deprivation of liberty.

The age of the child children and what is usual for them will be important issues when considering not only whether a deprivation of liberty is occurring but also whether those with PR could consent to any deprivation. This requires consideration of individual situations and circumstances. Whether it is adequate to rely on parental consent for a regime that amounts to a deprivation of liberty is likely to be subject to further consideration by the courts. Several cases show different outcomes on this issue and reflect both the very individual nature of each case, the age of the child and the specific role of those with PR. One must also bear in mind the Supreme Court ruling on what constitutes a deprivation of liberty, for example *RK; RK v BCC* [2011] and *Re D (A Child) (Deprivation of Liberty)* [2015]. Legal advice should be available to those who are required to take such decisions.

In some circumstances, Children Act provisions may be more appropriate than use of the MHA. In the case of *Re A* [2015], Justice Bodey made an interim secure accommodation order under s.25 Children Act 1989 in the case of a child where the criteria for s.2 MHA assessment were considered by CAMHS not to be fulfilled. However, the local authority maintained that A was 'a danger to herself and others and no longer containable in any form of ordinary residential unit'.

MCA and application to under 16s

The MCA may apply to those under 16 in relation to s.44 and the criminal offence of ill treatment or wilful neglect. The Court of Protection may also make an order related to the property and affairs of an under 16-year-old in certain circumstances (s.18(3)).

Compulsion in the community and deprivation of liberty

Compulsion in the community within the MHA does not authorise a deprivation of liberty, much as this has been discussed in particular in relation to guardianship (see Jones 2015).

However, those subject to guardianship, conditional discharge and CTOs can find themselves also subject to conditions/care plans that amount to a deprivation. In *Y County Council & ZZ* [2012], it was accepted that a DoLS authorisation could be given alongside guardianship as long as the DoLS did not conflict with the residence requirement.

Both the DoLS and guardianship order were necessary in this case as a result of ZZ's risk to the public and the management of this risk with the guardianship order.

In *KD v A Borough Council* [2015] the Upper-tier Tribunal explored the relationship between a guardianship order and DoLS authorisation. The authority of the guardian within s.7–s.8 to require a person to reside in a specified place cannot be over-ruled by the Court of Protection (*C v Blackburn and Darwen Borough Council* [2011]).

In the case of *PJ v A Local Health Board & Others* [2015], the Upper-tier Tribunal found that the First-tier Tribunal panel should have considered the full 'acid test' for deprivation of liberty. The Tribunal cannot disregard any breach of A5 ECHR created by the conditions of a CTO.

In *Secretary of State for Justice v KC and C Partnership NHS Foundation Trust* [2015], the Upper-tier Tribunal ruled that it was possible for a person to be conditionally discharged (s.37/s.41) from detention into conditions that amount to an 'objective' deprivation of liberty as long as this is lawfully authorised. In *MM v WL Clinic* [2015], the Tribunal took this further by ruling that a patient subject to a restriction order who had capacity could consent to conditions that amount to a deprivation of liberty. Obviously, the case looks closely at what consent might be and issues around withdrawal of consent.

On-the-spot question	When might an advance decision refusing treatment be over-ruled for a patient detained on section 3 MHA.

Further reading

Books and journals

Brown, R. A., P. Barber and D. Martin (2008) *The MCA: A Guide for Practice*, 2nd edn.

Cairns, R., P. Brown, H. Grant-Peterkin, M. Khondoker, G. Owen, G. Richardson, G. Szmukler et al. (2011) 'Judgements about Deprivation of Liberty Made by Various Professionals: Comparison Study'. This, among other research pieces, confirms the complexity of identifying a potential deprivation of liberty and the need for a review of the DoLS.

Department of Constitutional Affairs (2007) *Mental Capacity Act 2005 Code of Practice*. This guidance applies in England and Wales and offers clarity on applying the MCA in practice. Note that chapter 13 refers to the MHA prior to the 2007 amendments and is therefore out of date.

Department of Health (2015b) *Response to the Law Commission's Consultation on Mental Capacity and Deprivation of Liberty.*

The Law Society (2015) *Identifying a Deprivation of Liberty: A Practical Guide 2015*. The Law Society's helpful, practical guidance on identifying a deprivation of liberty is of value to anyone working in this field.

House of Commons Health Committee on the MCA 2005 (2014) *Post-legislative Scrutiny*. Helpful analysis of the MCA and its application in practice. A critique of the DoLS and the need for review.

Websites

www.39essex.com. The website of 39 Essex Street Chambers: monthly newsletters on MCA and case law, plus links to other newsletters and blogs.

www.mentalcapacitylawandpolicy.org.uk. This is a website run by Alex Ruck Keene, barrister at 39 Essex Chambers. Offering practical and up-to-date information and debate on MCA, MHA interface issues and the practical application of MCA and DoLS.

www.scie.org.uk/. This website has helpful information within the MCA Directory including MCA Rights cards and learning resources for social workers.

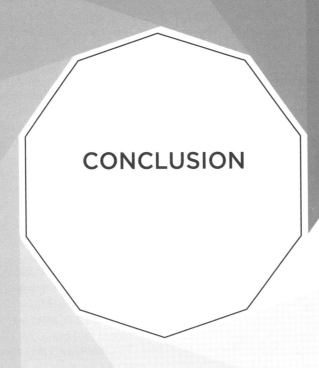

CONCLUSION

AT A GLANCE THIS CHAPTER COVERS:

♦ current and future policy and legal developments

Current and future policy and legal developments

There are many positive changes in the United Kingdom within mental health generally and the Time to Change National Attitudes Report of 2014 noted that public perceptions of mental health in England are changing for the better.

Successive governments have attempted to integrate recovery and empowerment agendas in their vision of what current mental health services should prioritise. The NHS England *Five-Year Forward View* (2014) and the Wales *Together for Mental Health – Strategy for Wellbeing in Wales* (2012) both refer to the development of services (including the involvement of third-sector agencies) that promote well-being and are accessible across ages. Improving Access to Psychological Services (IAPTS), the development of a Child and Young Person's Mental Health and Wellbeing Taskforce (NHS England), developments in perinatal mental health service delivery and strategies recognising the need to reduce stigma, improve well-being, enable more direct control to service users and increase preventative services, all read very positively.

Alongside this, the ongoing debate over 'parity of esteem' between physical and mental health care continues. As we have seen, reduction in bed availability alongside an increase in MHA detention rates (in particular in relation to black and black British groups) is part of a less positive picture. Mental health services are under 'unprecedented strain', and the 'gulf between rhetoric and reality threatens to leave vulnerable patients without vital support' (RCN 2014).

Transformation in health and social services makes it increasingly difficult for professionals and services users to negotiate mental health and social care services. The Cluster of Care model of mental health services, which separates services according to patient characteristics, as part of payment by results (NHS England 2014c) and which is currently used in many areas, reflects a medical model of care. This seems in contradiction to the move away from medicalisation and hospital-based care.

The NHS Act 2006 allows for partnership agreements between health and social services, to pool budgets and services (s.75). This led to the integrated multidisciplinary mental health services that many are familiar with. Social Services is the lead agency in the provision of social care, and the introduction of new community care legislation in England and Wales reflects principles of well-being which should feed into mental health service provision. Disaggregation of integrated mental health services in some areas may reflect the increasing demands on local authorities and their budgets which has led to social workers being removed from multidisciplinary mental health teams and budgets no longer being pooled. A lack of professional skill mix in mental health care provision has been referred to in the King's Fund Briefing 'Mental Health Under Pressure' (Gilbert 2015), which highlights that the 'scale of change is particularly notable'.

CPA and the role of the CC focus on generic skills and tasks for all mental health professionals. However, social workers take a lead role in adult and child safeguarding and should lead the way in promoting the social aspects of mental health care. The low morale of mental health social workers may reflect, in part, their reported experience of feeling de-professionalised and denigrated in mental health services (Clifton and Thorley 2014, cited in Gilbert 2015). The Annual NHS Survey of 2014 shows the highest level of work-related stress in mental health social workers in the last decade; only 8 per cent of social work students having a placement in mental health services; and high pressure and low morale among social workers in integrated services (Gilbert 2015). At a time when social perspectives and whole-family approaches are vital, the retention and recruitment of social workers to work within mental health is especially important. It may be, however, that integrated mental health services will become a thing of the past.

Alongside these transformations in structure and policy is the increasingly complex world of mental health law. As we have seen, it is impossible to work in mental health services without knowledge of the MCA, DoLS and HRA; and competencies of AMHPs in particular include having a working knowledge of a wide range of legislation, policy and research.

Devolution in Wales and the associated differences in some aspects of mental health law increase the complexities for those working in services (particularly for those working across the English and Welsh borders).

Ongoing case law in relation to deprivation of liberty and the MCA have an impact on the MHA and its interpretation:

> Understanding the interface between the MHA and DOLS is becoming so complex for lawyers and the judiciary – let alone anyone else – that there must now be a growing concern as to whether the legislation in fact complies with the ECHR.
>
> (39 Essex Chambers 2013)

The Law Commission review of the DoLS may be welcome but may also introduce new law, which professionals will have to become acquainted with over time.

It has therefore become very difficult to keep abreast of the development of mental health and capacity law in England and Wales. Social workers, AMHPs and other mental health and social care professionals are not lawyers. However, they may feel increasingly as though they are expected to have that level of knowledge and understanding of the law. They must not forget to refer to their legal departments, and prompt legal advice should be available.

Among this complexity and change, there is no doubt that social perspectives, which are the core element of social work, must remain a key focus both of mental health practice and law if we are to progress the positive agendas cited above.

Further reading

Royal College of Nursing (2014) *Turning Back the Clock? RCN Report on Mental Health Services in the UK*, 2 December, www.nhsconfed. org/resources/2014/12/rcn-report-shows-mental-health-services-under-unprecedented-strain.

'Time to Change National Attitudes 2013 Report' (2013) Rethink Mental Illness, www.rethink.org/get-involved/campaigns/time-to-change/time-to-change-national-attitudes-2013-report. The Time to Change campaign noted that public perceptions of mental health are changing for the better.

APPENDIX A

Table A.1: ECHR Articles Relevant to Mental Health

KEY ARTICLES	SOME RELEVANT CASES
A.2 – Right to life – everyone's right to life shall be protected by law.	***Savage v South Essex Partnership NHS Foundation Trust* [2008] UKHL** *'Hospitals have an operational obligation to protect the life of a detained patient who presents a "real and immediate risk" of suicide.'* ***Rabone v Pennine Care NHS Trust* [2012]** *'Positive obligation may be owed to an informal patient if the Trust failed to take steps that it could reasonably have been expected to take in light of the real risk.'*
A3 – No one shall be subject to torture or inhuman or degrading treatment or punishment.	***HA (Nigeria) v Secretary of State for Home Department* [2012] EWHC 979 (Admin)** *'A failure to take reasonably available measures which could have a real prospect of altering the outcome or mitigating the harm is sufficient to engage the responsibility of the state.'* In relation to a man with paranoid schizophrenia, held in an immigration detention centre despite medical recommendations for urgent transfer to hospital. Spent long periods in isolation, sleeping on floor, often naked, in the toilet area, drank and washed from toilet and was 'grossly unkempt'. ***MS v UK-ECtHR* [2012]** MS was held for more than 72 hours in police custody on s.136, MHA, despite two medical recommendations for his detention under the MHA. Banging his head on wall, drinking from toilet, smearing himself with faeces. In need of treatment.

(continued)

Table A.1: *Continued*

A5(1) – Everyone has the right to liberty and security of person. No one shall be deprived of his liberty save in the following cases and accordance with a procedure prescribed by law.	*HL v UK ECHR* (2004) Informal admission of an incapacitated, compliant patient was, on the facts, a deprivation of liberty. Not in accordance with a procedure prescribed by law and unable to appeal, hence A5(1) and (4) breached.
A5(4) – Everyone who is deprived of his liberty by arrest or detention shall be entitled to take proceedings by which the lawfulness of his detention shall be decided speedily by a court and his release ordered if the detention is not lawful.	*MH v UK 11577/06 ECHR 1008* (2013) In relation to her section 2 detention, the applicant, due to incapacity, could not 'take proceedings' of the kind guaranteed to her by A5(4).
A6 – Everyone is entitled to a fair and public hearing within a reasonable time by an independent and impartial Tribunal established by law.	*RM v St Andrew's Healthcare* [2010] **UKUT 119 (AAC)** The patient's Article 6 right to a fair hearing outweighed the risks to his physical and mental health of disclosing that he was being covertly medicated. The patient could not effectively challenge his detention without disclosure of the information.
A8(1) – Everyone has the right to respect for his private and family life, his home and correspondence.	*L B Hillingdon v Neary* [2011] EWHC **1377(COP)** In removing Steven, insufficient regard was paid to A8 ECHR.
A8(2) – There shall be no interference by a public authority with the exercise of this right expect such as in accordance with the law and is necessary.	*TW v Enfield [EWCA Civ 362, 2014]* When an [AMHP] is considering whether it is 'reasonably practicable' to consult the nearest relative before making an application (for admission) ... s.11(4) imposes an obligation on the AMHP to 'strike a balance between the patient's A5 right not to be detained unlawfully and the patient's A8 right to respect for private and family life'.

	R (Munjaz) v Mersey Care NHS Trust [2005] UKHL 58 The Code of Practice is statutory guidance, and cogent reasons are needed for departing from it. The use of seclusion need not breach Article 8 if governed by robust local policies. *R(N) v Secretary of State for Health* [2009] EWCA 795 There is no A8 right to smoke – and even if there were such a right, it would be lawful for Parliament to interfere with it by banning smoking in psychiatric hospitals, even if the result was that P would be entirely prevented from smoking.
A14 – Prohibition of discrimination – the enjoyment of the rights and freedoms set forth in this Convention shall be secured without discrimination on any grounds such as sex, race, colour, language, religion, political or other opinion, national or social origin, association with a national minority, property, birth or other status.	This is not a freestanding right but may be argued alongside a claim for a breach of another Convention right.

APPENDIX B

Using Jones' Mental Health Act manual

Jones' manual contains the Mental Health Act 1983, extracts from the Code of Practice to the MHA and Rules, Regulations, Circulars and Guidance along with Jones' own commentary. The 2015 edition of the manual is number 18, but it is regularly updated. Jones includes a table of cases (case law), which he refers to throughout the manual.

Using Jones' manual

The MHA is divided into *parts.* There are nine parts in all. If you look at Part VII, you will see that this has been repealed. These parts are then divided into sections, for example Section 18. The sections are divided into subsections, for example Section 18(1) and paragraphs, for example Section 18(1)(a).

Task: **Go through the contents of the Act and identify what each part includes. Look at Part VII – what was this and why has this been repealed?** You may notice at points that some paragraphs are within square brackets, that is [words, words, words]. This indicates text that has been amended. If the brackets are empty but have […] this indicates points where text has been repealed.

Task: **Look at section 25A and 3(2)(b) – can you identify what has happened to these sections and why?** At the top of each page of the Act, you will see the number c20. This denotes the running number given to Acts that were passed in that year. The middle top of each page gives the section number, which can be a quick route to finding what you need.

The wrongful use of the term *sectioned* actually refers to the fact that someone is subject to the powers of a particular paragraph/section of the legislation. It does not always mean 'detained'; for example, think about someone in the community subject to guardianship or a CTO.

Within Jones' manual you will see that legislation is written first and usually followed with a subheading in smaller font size, called *'General Notes'*. These notes are not the actual statute, but are Jones' comments on the statute, information and sources of repeals, amendments and references to relevant case law. He often cross-references within these notes and uses a paragraph numbering system at the side of the page to help you locate other notes, for example 1-020. These relate to the contents of the manual as a whole and are rather confusingly termed parts, so part 1 relates to the MHA, part 2 to delegated legislation, part 3 to practice and procedure, part 4 to guidance (such as the Code), part 5 to the Human Rights Act 1998, part 6 to deprivations of liberty and then several annexes. You can see this list in the contents page at the front of the Jones manual.

Task: Find 1-018 and note what this is. There is also an index at the back of the manual, and you will see that Jones does not use page numbers (because some notes span so many pages), but the numbering system as above, for example 1-018.

Following on from the actual text of the MHA, Jones has included extracts from the *Code of Practice*. Although the Code is arranged in sections, it is not referenced by section. The Code is referenced by chapters and paragraphs, for example chapter 3, para 1 or para 3.1, and so on. Jones also uses his numbering system at the side of the page.

Note in the *Table of Cases* that these are listed in alphabetical order. However, when you reach the letter 'R', you will notice that there is also an alphabetical list for all cases starting with R. It is worth searching within R for a piece of case law, even when the case may be known by a different name, In these cases, R stands for the Crown (Rex or Regina).

Schedules are appendices to an Act of Parliament.

Regulations are delegated legislation. Parliament passes the Act, but the 'how to' or the detail is left up to the Secretary of State.

Local authority circulars (LACs) and health circulars (HCs) are guidance and indicate the way the government wish to see the legislation implemented.

This exercise was written by the authors in 2006 for use on the Bournemouth University ASW qualifying course. It continues to be used on AMHP qualifying courses and in training run by Edge Training and Consultancy Ltd. It is also of more general use in reading law.

APPENDIX C

Welsh Law and the Welsh Assembly

The MHA applies in England and Wales. However, it is necessary to acknowledge some differences between the two countries.

UK Parliament remains sovereign and still legislates in areas relating to Wales. However, the Government of Wales Act 1998 and 2006 sets out areas of devolved responsibility to the Welsh Assembly. As a result, the Welsh Assembly has powers to make 'Measures' (Welsh Law) in some areas (e.g. the Mental Health Wales Measure 2010, which includes some variation in the provision of IMHA services in Wales).

Areas that have been devolved include health and social welfare, hence the Social Services and Wellbeing (Wales) Act 2014.

If Parliament wishes to legislate for any devolved areas of practice, the memorandum of understanding, 2011, requires its members to obtain consent of the Welsh Assembly through a 'Legislative Consent Motion'.

The Welsh Language Act 1993 established that Welsh should be treated on an equal basis with the English language in the public sector. The Welsh Code of Practice to the MHA is available in the Welsh language and makes reference to Welsh speakers in its principles at para 1.18.

The Social Services and Wellbeing (Wales) Act 2014

The Social Services and Wellbeing Act (Wales) 2014 was given Royal Assent in 2014 and is coming fully into force in 2016. This Act will change the law and create a new legal framework for Social Services in Wales. In parts, it is similar to the English Care Act 2014 but has different eligibility criteria and applies to all people regardless of age, including changes to 'children in need' and a 'repeal of some parts of the Children Act in Wales'. For more information on this, see www.lukeclements.co.uk.

Note that, in relation to Social Services duties, s.47 of the Care Act 2014 and protection of moveable property is s.58 of the Social Services and Wellbeing (Wales) Act 2014 (once it is in force).

www.assembly.wales. This website gives a really helpful outline of the history to devolution as well as the role that the national assembly play and the role of Welsh Government, and links with UK Parliament and Government.

A list of the main differences in mental health law and guidance between England and Wales

As the MHA applies in England and Wales, it is important to note some differences in the provision of services and aspects of the law. Be aware that regulations, guidance and polices do change. At present, the rate of change can seem overwhelming, and it is likely that there will be further change in the life of this book. It is important to keep abreast of the changes that are relevant to you. See some of the websites below for more details.

Table C.1: Differences between English and Welsh Provisions – Summary

	Wales	England
Code of Practice to MHA – S.118 places a duty on the Secretary of State for Health and Welsh ministers to prepare, publish and from time to time revise a code of practice. Wales and England have separate Codes of Practice.	The Welsh Code was published in November 2008 and is under revision at the time of writing. Note that Wales also currently has separate 'Good Practice Guidance', dated 2012 in relation to s.135 and s.136. This can be accessed at www. cymru.gov.uk.	The English Code was published in 2008, and the current revised version in April 2015.
Reference Guide – gives details of legal provisions, rather than guidance. There is cross-referencing to the English Code of Practice.	There is no separate Reference Guide for Wales, and the Reference Guide refers to the Act as it applies in England.	Current Reference Guide was revised and published in 2015 to coincide with the revised Code of Practice.

(continued)

Table C.1: *Continued*

S.130 – Independent Mental Health Advocates	S.130E–L. Wales makes provision for IMHAs to be available to a wider range of qualifying patients, including some informal patients. The variations in Wales were inserted by the Mental Health (Wales) Measure 2010. See also the Welsh Government guidance 2011: Delivering the Independent Mental Health Advocacy Service in Wales: Guidance for Independent Mental Health Advocacy Providers and Local Health Board Advocacy Service Planners.	S.130A–D details who is a 'qualifying patient' for the IMHA service, what that service includes and which national authority is responsible for providing these. The Mental Health (Independent Advocacy) (England) Bill 2015–16 proposes changes to this.
Aftercare in s.117, MHA	The changes to s.117 by the Care Act need to be read with reference to the Social Services and Wellbeing (Wales) Act 2014.	There are specific changes to s.117 made by the Care Act 2014.
Section 114 – AMHP Competencies as set out in Regulations. These vary between England and Wales. It is therefore not automatic that approval as an AMHP in England would meet with approval in Wales.	The Mental Health (Approval of Persons to be Approved Mental Health Professionals) (Wales) Regulations 2008 Statutory Instrument no. 2436 (W 209) 2008 (Wales).	AMHP Competencies in regulations The Mental Health (Approved Mental Health Professionals) (Approval) (England) Regulations 2008 Statutory Instrument no. 1206 2008 (England).

Approved clinicians (s.145 sets out the definition). Also s.142A – mutual recognition of approval as an AC in England and Wales.	National Health Service (Wales) Act – MHA 1983 Approved Clinician (Wales) Directions 2008 – Schedule 2 sets out the relevant AC competencies.	Section 12ZA sets out the approving body in England. National Health Service Act – MHA 1983 Approved Clinician (General) (England) Directions 2008 – Schedule 2 sets out the relevant AC competencies.
Mental Health Regulations 1983. These set out the details of statutory forms used in the MHA.	Welsh statutory forms can be accessed from www.wales.nhs.uk.	English statutory forms can be accessed from www.mentalhealthlaw.co.uk.
Care Programme Approach	CPA – Mental Health (Wales) Measure parts 1 & 2.	CPA and refocusing the CPA (gateway ref 9148) 2008. Department of Health.
Establishment of Mental Health (Review) Tribunals	Part V of the MHA, s.65, and various schedules provide for the Mental Health Review Tribunal (Tribunal for Wales). Section 78 deals with the procedure of the tribunal in Wales.	The English Mental Health Tribunal system (named the First-tier Tribunal (Mental Health)) is established by the Tribunal, Courts & and Enforcement Act 2007. Both tribunals have identical powers and duties. The details of these are set out from s.66 onwards.

(*continued*)

Table C.1: *Continued*

Annual statistics on the use of the MHA	Welsh Government website (www.gov. wales) holds annual statistics on the use of the MHA in Wales. See May 2015 for a revised report on admissions and CTOs.	Statistics on the use of the MHA in England are at the Health and Social Care Information Centre and are usually published in October of each year, www. hscic.gov.uk.
NHS structures between Wales and England differ. The MHA may refer to CCG or LHB. See explanation.	Local health board Wales. There are seven LHBs in Wales and three NHS Trusts. This includes a Welsh ambulance service. For more information, go to www.wales.nhs.uk.	Clinical commissioning groups and NHS England The current structure in England is based on clinical commissioning groups for each area (taking over from the previous primary care trusts [PCTs]). CCGs commission health services for their area. NHS England is responsible for commissioning specialist services, offender healthcare and some services for the armed forces, www. england.nhs.uk.
Health inspection organisations	Health Inspectorate Wales (HIW) is responsible for the inspection and regulation of Welsh NHS services (including Welsh NHS funded care) and independent healthcare services in Wales. They do so on behalf of the Welsh ministers, www.hiw. org.uk.	Care Quality Commission is the independent regulator of health and adult social care in England, www.cqc.org.uk. Ofsted undertake the regulation of children's services, www.ofsted. gov.uk.

Social Services inspection organisations	The Care and Social Services Inspectorate for Wales (CCSIW) is responsible for inspection and regulation of social and non-health care for adults and children in Wales. It does so on behalf of the Welsh ministers, www.cssiw.org.uk.	As above.
Social work registration bodies This is a devolved matter and therefore varies between England and Wales. It is important for social workers working across both countries to ensure they meet the requirements of registration as they apply in both countries.	Care Council for Wales is responsible for the registration of social workers in Wales, www.ccwales.org.uk.	Health Care Professionals Council is responsible for the registration of social workers in England, www.hpc-uk.org.

Some relevant Welsh policy and guidance in relation to mental health

Royal College of Psychiatrists: College Report (CR)195 – When to see a child and adolescent psychiatrist.

Together for Mental Health Annual Report 2013–14: Welsh Government. Pub: February 2015.

Addressing Mental Health Problems of Children and Young People in the Youth Justice System: Welsh Government and Youth Justice Board. Pub: 2014.

Health and Social Care Committee – Alcohol and Substance Misuse: National Assembly for Wales. Pub: August 2015.

Health Standards Framework: Welsh Government. Pub: January 2015.

Talk to Me 2: Consultation on the draft 'Suicide and Self Harm Prevention Strategy and Action Plan for Wales: Welsh Government. Pub: March 2015.

The Thematic Review of Deaths of Children and Young People through Probable Suicide in Wales: Public Health Wales. Pub: March 2014.

GLOSSARY

Assertive outreach teams
Specialist multidisciplinary mental health teams working with adult patients between ages 18 and 65 (upper age limits may vary in each locality). These teams were set up to implement the Government's assertive outreach model. The Policy Implementation Guide (DH 2001) described the service as for those with a severe and persistent mental disorder, a history of high use of in-patient or intensive home-based care, difficulty in maintaining lasting and consenting contact with services, and multiple complex needs. In many areas, these teams have now been disbanded, and the assertive outreach approach may be integrated into generic mental health teams.

AWOL
Absent without leave. For those subject to certain sections and who require s.17 leave, absenting themselves without the necessary leave.

CAMHS
Child and adolescent mental health services. Multidisciplinary teams working with children up to the age of 18 years. Referral to these teams would usually come via the general practitioner but also from schools, health visitors, social services, or youth counselling, etc. There is no lower age limit for CAMHS, although it is seen as a specialist service so usually sees children or young people where there are specific concerns about their emotional/psychological well-being.

Capacity
Any reference to capacity within the text can be read as capacity within the meaning of the MCA 2005.

Community mental health teams (CMHTs)
Multidisciplinary teams working with adults of at least 18 years and usually up to 65 years. Adults over 65 are generally treated by older adult mental health teams. Those under the care of the CMHT are likely to be under the Care Programme Approach and have a care coordinator. CMHTs may now

be organised as brief treatment or intake teams, followed by recovery teams for longer-term work and specialist teams for those with personality disorders or psychotic disorders. There may also be rehabilitation teams. This is a fast-changing landscape.

Crisis resolution and home treatment teams (CRHT)

Set up by Government to provide 24-hour access seven days a week to support those between 16 and 65 years (although local services' age limits may vary). Support is provided in an acute psychiatric crisis and aims to minimise the need for admission to hospital by offering support and containment at home. This is in line with the principle of least restriction. For those where admission is necessary, this team can be actively engaged in discharge planning to enable early discharge. These teams may also be the 'gatekeeper' for admission to psychiatric hospital bed availability.

Duty

The Oxford Dictionary of Law defines this as a legal requirement to carry out or refrain from carrying out an act.

Early intervention teams

Early intervention teams were set up by the Government to provide particular support to people experiencing a first episode of psychosis. Originally the service was aimed at people between ages 14 and 35, but this is variable in services now. These are multidisciplinary teams – in many places now disbanded, so the approach should be integrated into generic mental health teams.

Forensic

Relating to courts of law. Commonly used to denote services dealing with patients subject to Part III, MHA.

Inherent jurisdiction of the High Court

A doctrine developed by case law which permits higher courts to deal with *any* issue that arises in proceedings unless expressly limited or prevented by a statute. In practice, the jurisdiction has been invoked to take steps to protect vulnerable children or adults, for example by making injunctions against third parties. The Mental Capacity Act has superseded this common law power in respect of incapacitated adults.

Liable to be detained

When a patient is subject to an application under Part II duly made or court order under Part III, but prior to being accepted at a hospital.

Multidisciplinary teams

Within mental health services, this refers to a team of professionals such as doctors, psychologists, nurses, social workers, occupational therapists and others who are based and work together.

Power

A legal provision authorising certain acts and sometimes referred to as 'can' do; different from a duty which is often referred to as a 'must' do.

Risk

The probability of negative or positive outcomes. Often used as a phrase to denote criteria within the MHA or in policy to denote the management of mental disorder and negative consequences for the person or public.

Safeguards

Commonly used in mental health and human rights law to refer to safeguards against arbitrary detention, hence the Deprivation of Liberty Safeguards. The MHA safeguards include the assessment process for admission, the roles of mental health tribunal and hospital managers, and the nearest relative. Patients' statutory rights, second opinion appointed doctors and Part IV rules on consent to treatment and inspection organisations provide additional safeguards against abuse.

Safeguarding

A term found within policies meant to protect vulnerable adults and in the Care Act and Health and Social Services Wellbeing (Wales) Act 2014. The phrase is also used in relation to safeguarding children.

Scope of parental responsibility

A term used in the MHA English Code of Practice to define when decisions regarding treatment or admission in respect of a child or young person might be made by persons with parental responsibility.

BIBLIOGRAPHY

39 Essex Chambers (2013) 'When Is Detention Under MHA 1983 'Necessary' for Incapacitated Adults?' *Mental Capacity Law Newsletter*, 37.

Adams, R., L. Dominelli and M. Payne (2002) *Critical Practice in Social Work*, 2nd edn (Basingstoke: Palgrave Macmillan).

ADASS (2015) *Transforming Care for People with Learning Disabilities – Next Steps* (London: ADASS).

Administrative Justice and Tribunals Council and Care Quality Commission (2011) *Patients' Experiences of the First-tier Tribunal (Mental Health)* (AJTC and CQC).

Allen, R. (2014) *The Role of the Social Worker in Adult Mental Health Services* (London: The College of Social Work).

American Psychiatric Association (2015) *Diagnostic and Statistical Manual of Mental Disorders*, 5th edn, www.psychiatry.org/psychiatrists/practice/dsm/dsm-5, accessed 4 July 2015.

Bartlett, P. and R. Sandland (2014) *Mental Health Law: Policy and Practice*, 4th edn (Oxford: OUP).

Bracken, P. and P. Thomas (2004) 'Postpsychiatry is not another Model', *Openmind*, 125: 6–7.

Brown, R., P. Barber and D. Martin (2008) *The Mental Capacity Act – A Guide for Practice*, 2nd edn. (Exeter: Learning Matters).

Brown, R., P. Barber and D. Martin (2009) *Mental Health Law in England and Wales – A Guide for Mental Health Professionals* (London: Sage).

Brown, R. (2009) *The Approved Mental Health Professional's Guide to Mental Health Law*, 2nd edn (Exeter: Sage).

Brown, R. (2013) *The Approved Mental Health Professional's Guide to Mental Health Law*, 3rd edn (London: Sage).

Burns, T. et al. (2013) 'Community Treatment Orders for Patients with Psychosis (OCTET): A Randomised Controlled Trial', *The Lancet*, 381(9878): 1627–33.

Cairns, R. et al. (2011) 'Judgements about Deprivation of Liberty Made by Various Professionals: Comparison Study', *Psychiatrist*, 35: 344–9.

Care Council for Wales (2015) *The Social Worker Practice Guidance.*

Care Quality Commission (2010) *Monitoring the Mental Health Act in 2008/09. CQC 2015. Report pursuant to section 120D(3) of the MHA* (Newcastle: CQC).

Care Quality Commission (2014) *Monitoring the Mental Health Act in 2012/13. CQC 2015. Report pursuant to section 120D(3) of the MHA* (Newcastle: CQC).

Care Quality Commission (2015a) *National Summary of the Results of the 2014 Community Mental Health Survey* (Newcastle: CQC).

Care Quality Commission (2015b) *Monitoring the Mental Health Act in 2013/14. Report pursuant to section 120D(3) of the MHA* (Newcastle: CQC).

Churchill, R., D. Owen, S. Singh and M. Hotopf (2007) *International Experiences of Using Community Treatment Orders* (London: IOP).

The Commission to Review the Provision of Acute Inpatient Psychiatric Care for Adults (2015) *Improving Acute Inpatient Psychiatric Care for Adults in England – Interim Report* (London: Commission on Acute Adult Psychiatric Care).

Department of Health (1992) *Review of Health and Social Services for Mentally Disordered Offenders and Others Requiring Similar Services: Final Summary Report (The Reed Report)* (London: Her Majesty's Stationery Office).

Department of Health (1993) *Legal Powers on the Care of Mentally Ill People in the Community. Report of the Internal Review* (London: Her Majesty's Stationery Office).

Department of Health (1999a) *Review of the Mental Health Act 1983* (London: Her Majesty's Stationery Office).

Department of Health (1999b) *National Service Framework for Mental Health – Modern Standards and Service Models* (London: Her Majesty's Stationery Office).

Department of Health (1999c) *Reform of the Mental Health Act 1983: Proposals for Consultation* (London: Her Majesty's Stationery Office).

Department of Health (2000) *Reforming the Mental Health Act* (London: Her Majesty's Stationery Office).

Department of Health (2001) *The Mental Health Policy Implementation Guide* (London: DH).

Department of Health (2002) *Draft Mental Health Bill 2002* (London: DH).

Department of Health (2004a) *Draft Mental Health Bill 2004* (London: DH).

Department of Health (2004b) *The Ten Essential Shared Capabilities – A Framework for the Whole of the Mental Health Workforce* (London: DH).

Department of Health (2007) *Best Practice in Managing Risk* (London: DH).

Department of Health (2008) *Refocusing the Care Programme Approach. Policy and Positive Practice Guidance* (London: DH).

Department of Health (2009) *The Bradley Report – Lord Bradley's Review of People with Mental Health Problems or Learning Disabilities in the Criminal Justice System* (London: DH).

Department of Health (2011) *No Health Without Mental Health – A Cross-Government Mental Health Outcomes Strategy for People of all Ages* (London: DH).

Department of Health (2012) *Transforming Care – A National Response to Winterbourne View Hospital* (London: DH).

Department of Health (2014a) *Mental Health Crisis Care Concordat – Improving Outcomes for People Experiencing Mental Health Crisis* (London: DH).

Department of Health (2014b) *Achieving Better Access to Mental Health Services by 2020* (London: DH).

Department of Health, Home Office, The Rt Hon Damien Green and The Rt Hon Norman Lamb (2014c) *Review of the Operation of Sections 135 and 136 Mental Health Act 1983 – Review Report and Recommendations* (London: DH).

Department of Health (2014d) *Valuing Every Voice, Respecting Every Right: Making the Case for the Mental Capacity Act* (London: DH).

Department of Health (2015a) *No Voice Unheard, No Right Ignored – A Consultation for People with Learning Disabilities, Autism and Mental Health Conditions* (London: DH).

Department of Health (2015b) *Response to the Law Commission's Consultation on Mental Capacity and Deprivation of Liberty*, 11 December (London: DH).

Edgar, K. and D. Rickford (2009) *Too Little Too Late: An Independent Review of Unmet Mental Health Need in Prison* (London: Prison Reform Trust).

Eldergill, A. (1997) *Mental Health Review Tribunals: Law and Procedure* (London: Sweet and Maxwell).

Fennell, P, P. Letts and J. Wilson (2013) *Mental Health Tribunals* (London: The Law Society).

Fernando, S. (2010) 'Ethnic Research – Whose Benefit?', 2 January, www.sumanfernando.com, accessed 12 March 2016.

Flynn, M. and V. Citarella (2012) *South Gloucestershire Safeguarding Adults Board – Winterbourne View Hospital – A Serious Case Review* (Bristol: CPEA).

Gilbert, P. (2010) *The Value of Everything – Social Work and its Importance in the Field of Mental Health*, 2nd edn (Lyme Regis: Russell House).

Gilburt, H., E. Peck, B. Ashton, N. Edwards and C. Naylor (2014) *Ideas that Change Health Care – Service Transformation – Lessons from Mental Health* (London: King's Fund).

Gilburt, H. (2015) *Mental Health Under Pressure – King's Fund Briefing* (London: King's Fund).

Golightley, M. (2014) *Social Work and Mental Health*, 5th edn (London: Sage).

Gostin, L., P. Bartlett, P. Fennell, J. McHale and R. Mackay (eds) (2010) *Principles of Mental Health Law and Policy* (Oxford: OUP).

Hale, B. (2010) *Mental Health Law*, 5th edn (London: Sweet and Maxwell).

Hardy, S., R. Kramer, G. Holt, P. Woodward and E. Chaplin (2006) *Supporting Complex Needs: A Practical Guide for Support Staff Working with People with a Learning Disability Who Have Mental Health Needs* (London: Turning Point and Estia).

Health and Care Professions Council (2012) *Standards of Proficiency – Social Workers in England.*

Health Inspectorate Wales (2015) *Monitoring the Use of the Mental Health Act in 2013/14. Report pursuant to section 120D(4).* (Merthyr Tydfil: HIW).

Health and Social Care Information Centre (2014) *Inpatients Formally Detained to Hospital under the Mental Health Act 1983 and Patients Subject to Supervised Community Treatment* (Annual Statistics 2013/2014) (Leeds: HSCIC).

Health and Social Care Information Centre (2015a) *Inpatients Formally Detained to Hospital under the Mental Health Act 1983 and Patients Subject to Supervised Community Treatment* (Annual Statistics 2014/2015) (Leeds: HSCIC).

Health and Social Care Information Centre (2015b) *Mental Capacity Act 2005, Deprivation of Liberty Safeguards (England), Annual Report 2014–15* (Leeds HSCIC).

Health and Social Care Information Centre (2015c) *Mental Health Bulletin: Annual Statistics 2014 to 2015* (Leeds: HSCIC)

Hewitt, D. (2009) *The Nearest Relative Handbook* (London: Jessica Kingsley).

Hewitt, D. (2013) 'Illegitimate Concern', *Solicitors Journal*, 157(25): 9.

House of Commons Health Committee (2014) *Post-legislative Scrutiny of the MHA 2007* (London: The Stationery Office).

House of Lords, Select Committee on the Mental Capacity Act 2005 (2014) *Mental Capacity Act 2005: Post-legislative Scrutiny* (London: The Stationery Office).

Hudson, J. and M. Webber (2012) *The National AMHP Survey 2012 – Final Report: Stress and the Statutory Role – Is There a Difference between Professional Groups?* (London: Kings College).

Hunt, I., M. Rahman, D. While, K. Windfuhr, J. Shaw, L. Appleby and N. Kapur (2014) 'Safety of Patients under the Care of Crisis Resolution Home Treatment Services in England: A Retrospective Analysis of Suicide Trends from 2003 to 2011', *The Lancet*, 1(2): 135–41.

Jones, R. (2015) *Mental Health Act Manual*, 18th edn (London: Thomson Reuters).

Law, J. and E. Martin (eds) (2009) *A Dictionary of Law* (Oxford: OUP).

Law Commission (2013) *Criminal Liability: Insanity and Automatism. A Discussion Paper* (London: Law Commission).

Law Society (2015) *Identifying a Deprivation of Liberty: A Practical Guide* (London: Law Society).

Lord Rix (2007) Hansard, vol. 688: col. 64.

Manthorpe, J. and J. Rapapport (2008) 'Family Matters: Developments Concerning the Role of the Nearest Relative and Social Workers under Mental Health Law in England and Wales', *British Journal of Social Work*, 38: 1115–31.

McConnell, P. and J. Talbot (2013) *Mental Health and Learning Disabilities in the Criminal Courts – Information for Magistrates, District Judges and Court Staff* (London: Prison Reform Trust and Rethink).

McNicoll, A. (2014) *Mental Health, Mental Health Act, The State of Mental Healthcare*, www.communitycare.co.uk/2014/11/28/deaths-linked-mental-health-beds-crisis-cuts-leave-little-slack-system/, accessed 2 October 2015.

Mencap (2007) *Death by Indifference – Following Up the Treat Me Right! Report* (London: Mencap).

Mental Health Act Commission (2008) *Risk, Rights and Recovery – 12th Biennial Report* (London: The Stationery Office).

Ministry of Justice (2009) *Guidance for Social Supervisors* (London: MoJ).

Ministry of Justice (2015) *Guidance for Working with MAPPA and Mentally Disordered Offenders* (London: MoJ).

Ministry of Justice – National Offender Management Service (2012) *Guidance for Working with MAPPA and Mentally Disordered Offenders* (London: MoJ).

Moriarty, J., M. Baginsky and J. Manthorpe (2015) *Literature Review of Roles and Issues within the Social Work Profession in England* (London: Kings College London & Social Care Workforce Research Unit).

National Institute for Health and Care Excellence (2003) *Guidance on the Use of Electroconvulsive Therapy*, Nice, April, www.nice.org.uk/guidance/ta59, accessed 12 March 2015.

National Institute for Mental Health in England (NIMHE) (2008) *Mental Health Act 2007 New Roles: Guidance for Approving Authorities and Employers on Approved Mental Health Professionals and Approved Clinicians* (London: National Institute for Mental Health in England). Gateway reference 19512.

NHS England (2009) *The Independent Inquiry into the Care and Treatment of Peter Bryan* (NHS England).

NHS England (2014a) *Background to the 2015/16 Proposals for the Mental Health Payment System* (London: NHS England).

NHS England (2014b) *Five-Year Forward View* (London: NHS England).

NHS England (2014c) *Liaison and Diversion – Standard Service Specification 2013/14* (London: NHS England).

Peay, J. (2015) *Sentencing Mentally Disordered Offenders: Conflicting Objectives, Perilous Decisions and Cognitive Insights* (London: LSE).

Perks, M. (2010) 'Appropriate Adult Provision in England and Wales', NAAN, www.appropriateadult.org.uk/images/survey2010.pdf, accessed 12 March 16.

Pilgrim, D. (2009) *Key Concepts in Mental Health*, 2nd edn (London: Sage).

Ritchie, J. et al. (1994) *The Report of the Inquiry into the Care and Treatment of Christopher Clunis* (London: The Stationery Office).

Rogers, A. and D. Pilgrim (2005) *A Sociology of Mental Health and Illness*, 3rd edn (Maidenhead: Open University Press).

Royal College of Nursing (2014) *Turning Back the Clock? RCN Report on Mental Health Services in the UK*, 2 December, www.nhsconfed. org/resources/2014/12/rcn-report-shows-mental-health-services-under-unprecedented-strain, accessed 12 March 2016.

Royal College of Psychiatrists (2011) *Do the Right Thing: How to Judge a Good Ward. 10 Standards for Adult In-patient Mental Healthcare – Occasional Paper OP79* (London: RCP).

Royal College of Psychiatrists (2013) *Guidance for Commissioners: Service Provision for Section 136 of the Mental Health Act 1983 – Position Statement PS2/2013* (London: RCP).

Royal College of Psychiatrists (2015) *Information about ECT*, www.rcpsych. ac.uk/healthadvice/treatmentswellbeing/ect.aspx, accessed 12 March 2016.

Sainsbury Centre for Mental Health (2009) *Diversion – A Better Way for Criminal Justice and Mental Health* (London: SCMH).

Scott-Moncrieff, L. and G. Vassall-Adams (2006) 'Insanity and Unfitness to Please – Yawning Gap', *Counsel*, October.

Silman, J. (2015) 'Social Worker Who Based Decisions on Family Views, Not Service Users, Suspended', Community Care, www.community care.co.uk/2015/06/03/social-worker-manage-dynamic-service-users-families-suspended/, accessed 12 March 2016.

Singh, S. and T. Burns (2006) 'Controversy – Race and Mental Health – There is More to Race than Racism', *British Medical Journal*, 333: 648–51.

Social Care Institute for Excellence (SCIE) (2012) 'At a Glance 9: Think Child, Think Parent, Think Family', May, www.scie.org.uk/publications/ ataglance/ataglance09.asp, accessed 12 March 2016.

Social Exclusion Unit (1997) *Social Exclusion Unit: Purpose, Work Priorities and Working Methods* (London: The Stationery Office).

Stein, G. and G. Wilkinson (eds) (2007) *Seminars in General Adult Psychiatry* (London: RCP).

Straw, J. (1999) Hansard, vol. 325: col. 601.

Stroud, J., K. Doughty and L. Banks (2013) *An Exploration of Service User and Practitioner Experiences of Community Treatment Orders* (Brighton: University of Brighton).

Time to Change (2008) 'Stigma Shout', www.time-to-change.org.uk, accessed 4 July 2015

Time to Change (2014) *Attitudes to Mental Illness Research Report*, www.rethink.org/media/1179746/Attitudes_to_mental_illness_2013_report.pdf, accessed 4 July 2015.

'Time to Change National Attitudes 2013 Report' (2013) Rethink Mental Illness, www.rethink.org/get-involved/campaigns/time-to-change/time-to-change-national-attitudes-2013-report, accessed 4 July 2015.

UK Government (2013) *Memorandum of Understanding and Supplementary Agreements between the United Kingdom Government, the Scottish Ministers, the Welsh Ministers, and the Northern Ireland Executive Committee* (London: The Stationery Office).

University of Manchester (2010) *The National Confidential Inquiry into Suicide and Homicide by People with Mental Illness Annual Report 2010: England, Northern Ireland, Scotland and Wales* (Manchester: University of Manchester).

University of Manchester (2015) *The National Confidential Inquiry into Suicide and Homicide by People with Mental Illness Annual Report 2015: England, Northern Ireland, Scotland and Wales* (Manchester: University of Manchester).

Watson, J. and S. Daley (2015) 'The Use of Section 135(1) of the Mental Health Act in a London Borough', *Mental Health Review Journal*, 20(3): 133–43.

Weaver, T. et al. (2003) 'Comorbidity of Substance Misuse and Mental Illness in Community Mental Health and Substance Misuse Services', *British Journal of Psychiatry*, 183: 304–13.

Welsh Government (2011) *Delivering the Independent Mental Health Advocacy Service in Wales: Guidance for Independent Providers and Local Health Board Advocacy Service Planners* (Cardiff: Welsh Government).

Welsh Government (2012a) *Mental Health Act 1983 – Sections 135 and 136 of the Mental Health Act 1983 – Good Practice Guidance* (Cardiff: Welsh Government).

Welsh Government (2012b) *Together for Mental Health – Strategy for Wellbeing in Wales* (Cardiff: Welsh Government).

Welsh Government (2015) *Admission of Patients to Mental Health Facilities* (Cardiff: Welsh Government).

Welsh Government and Department of Health (2015) *Mental Health Aftercare in England and Wales – Arrangements for Resolving Disputes over Ordinary Residence Involving Local Authorities in England and Wales.*

Wise, S. (2012) *Inconvenient People: Lunacy, Liberty, and the Mad-Doctors in England* (London: The Bodley Head).

World Health Organization (2015) *International Classification of Diseases and Related Health Problems*, 10th rev., apps.who.int/classifications/icd10/browse/2016/en, accessed 12 March 2016.

World Health Organization (n.d.) *Fact File – 10 Facts on Mental Health*. www.who.int/classifications/icd/factsheet/en/, accessed 12 March 2016.

INDEX